Coty

The Treasure

Coty's Adventures

Vol. 1

y: Tejveer Rathore

Illustrated by: Joseline C

Clever Fox® PUBLISHING
Chennai • Bangalore

OX PUBLISHING
dia

y CLEVER FOX PUBLISHING 2024

93-56487-81-9

Dedication

"To all animal lovers and children of the world,
especially the child we all carry within."

T&J

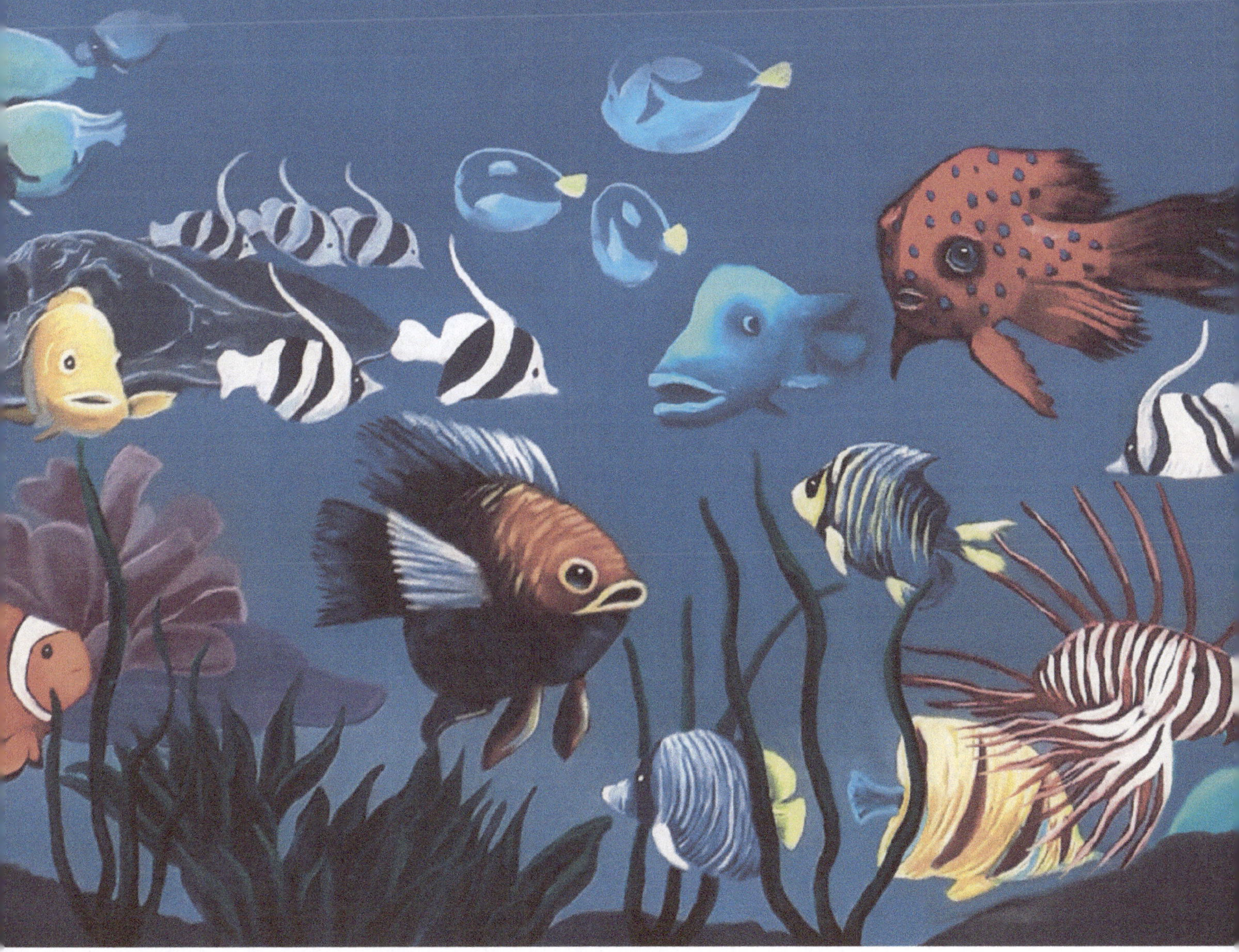

This is how the story flows...

On Nanao Island, there is Blue Bay.

Overlooking the bay, perched on a cliff, where the wind blows,

a colourful town with bright yellow flowers greets the beautiful sky.

The friendly folks living in town call themselves Nanoitos,

They enjoy breathtaking views and amazing sunsets from their cliff house

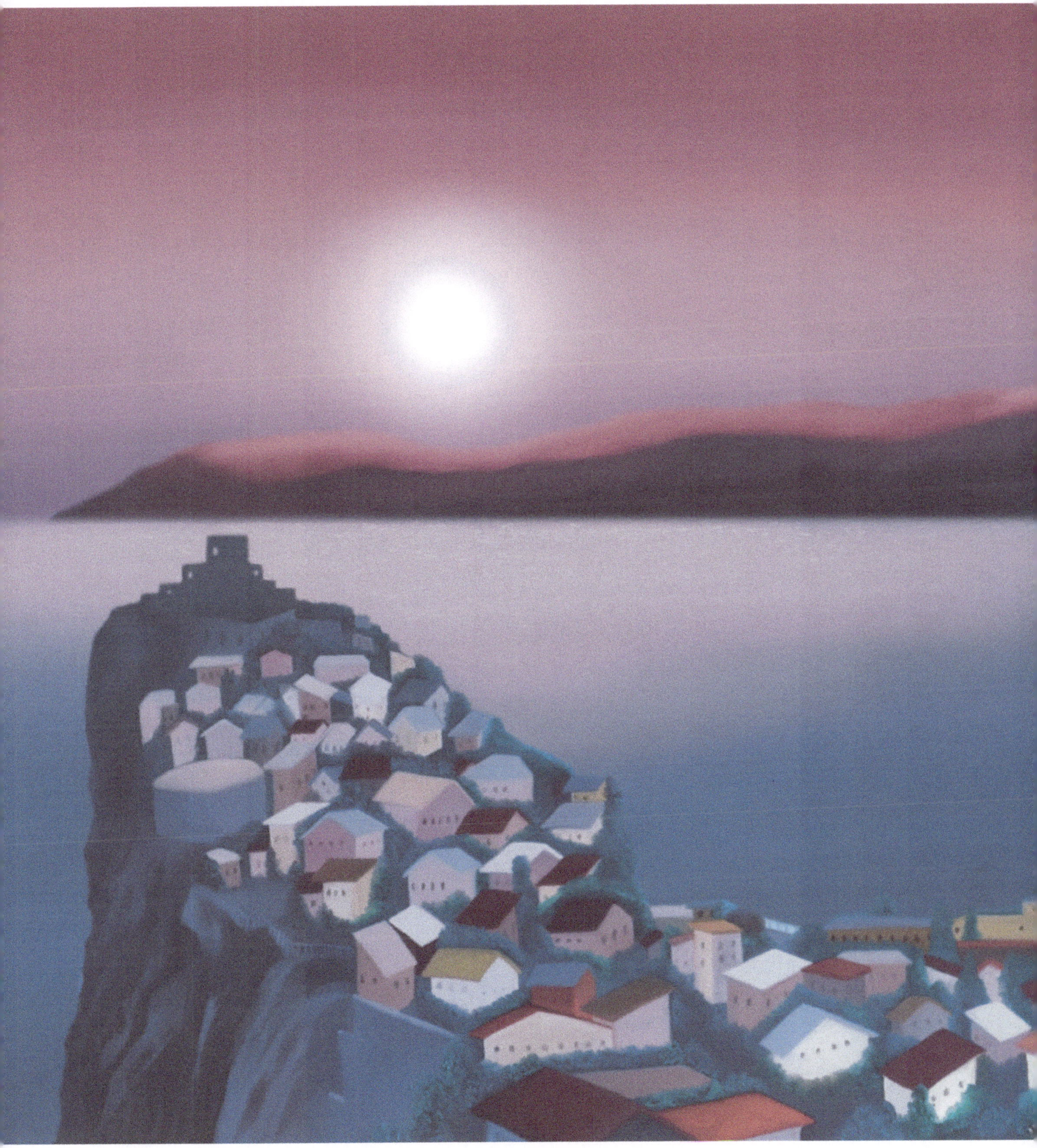

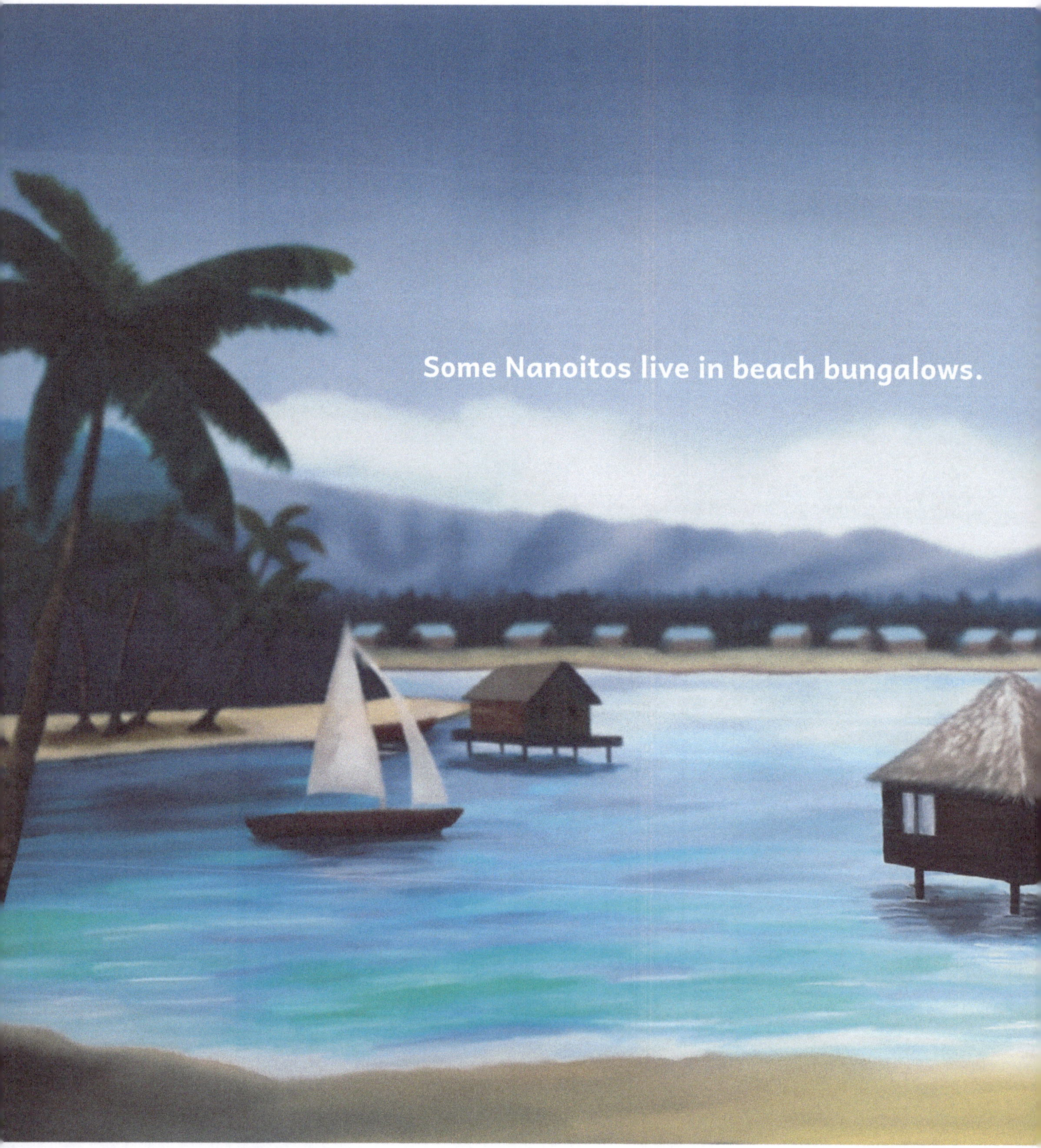
Some Nanoitos live in beach bungalows.

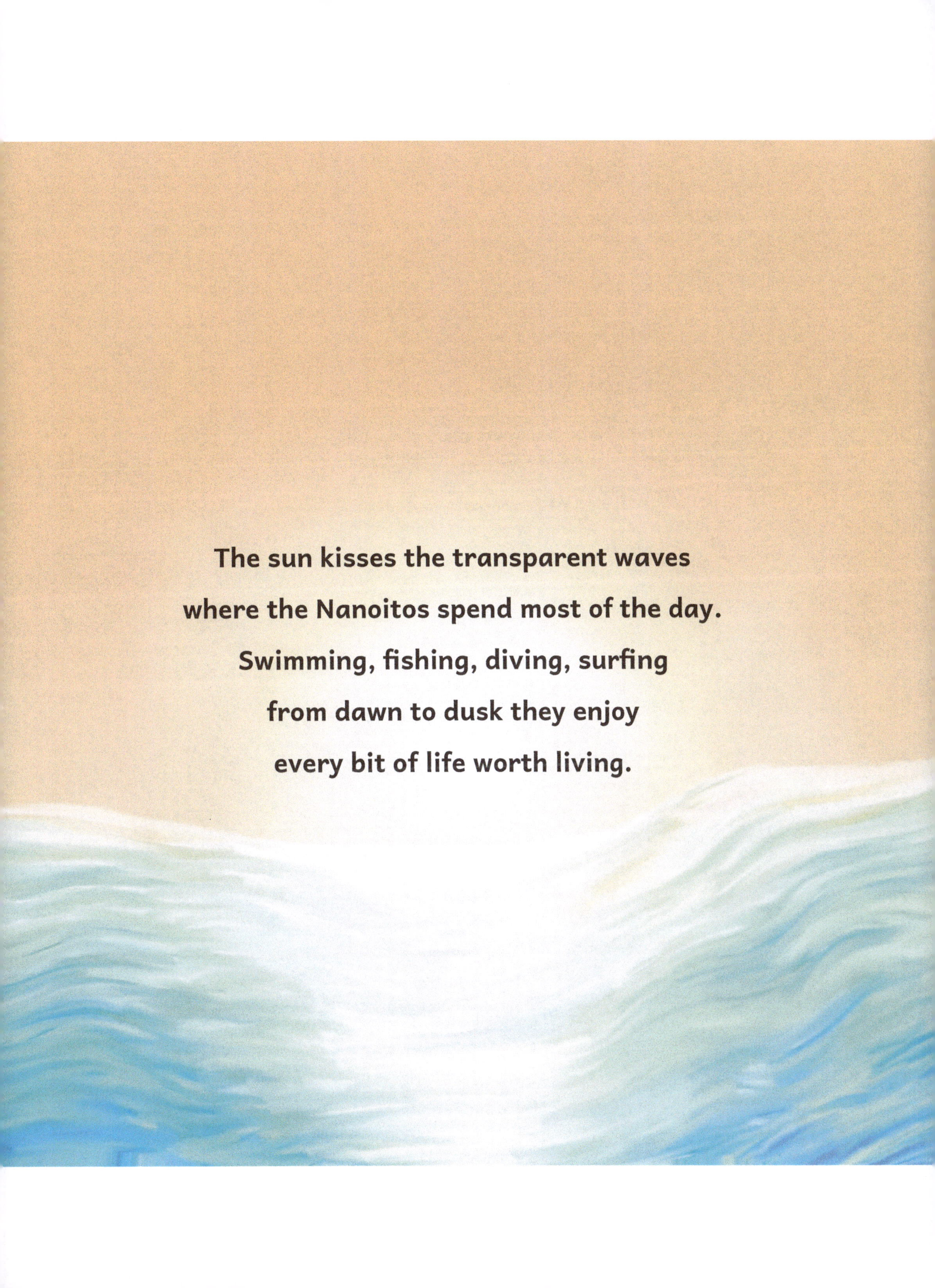

The sun kisses the transparent waves
where the Nanoitos spend most of the day.
Swimming, fishing, diving, surfing
from dawn to dusk they enjoy
every bit of life worth living.

But the real magic is not above but below
the surface of the sea...

Hidden below is a coral reef where species of vibrant
colors and different sizes live in harmony.

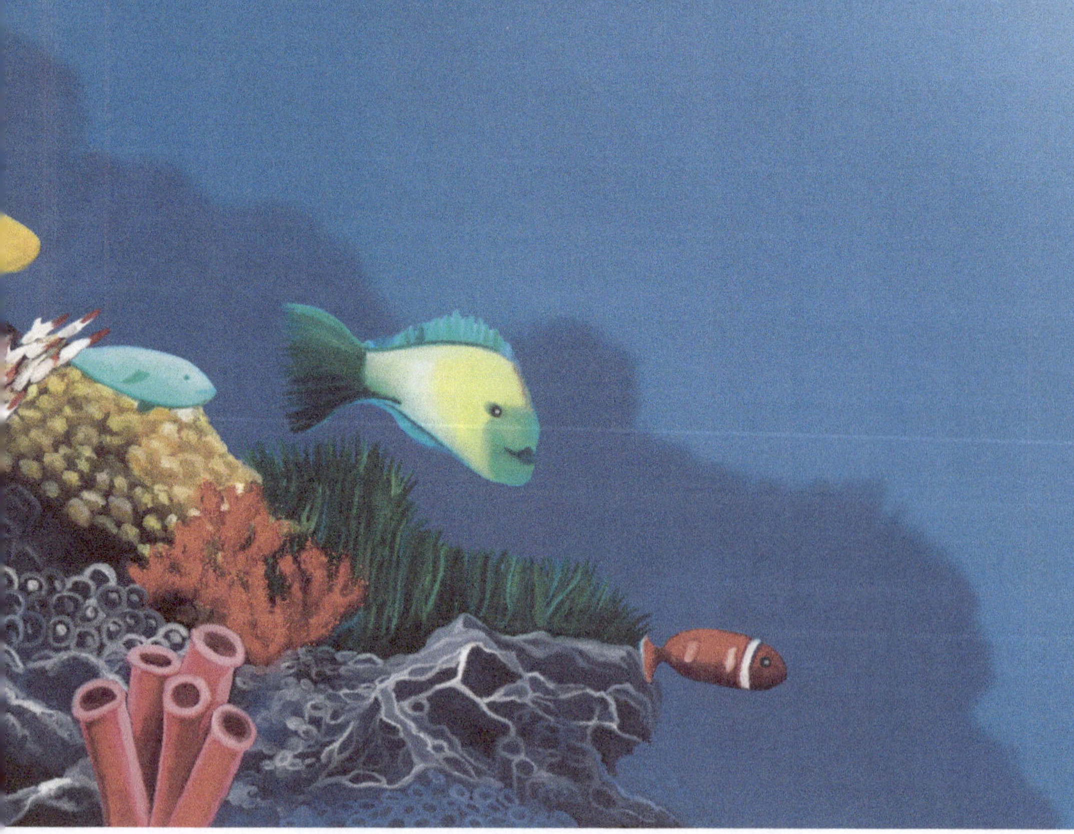

Schools of little fish

meet to play hide and seek.

Sometimes they discover a

precious pearl inside a sea shell.

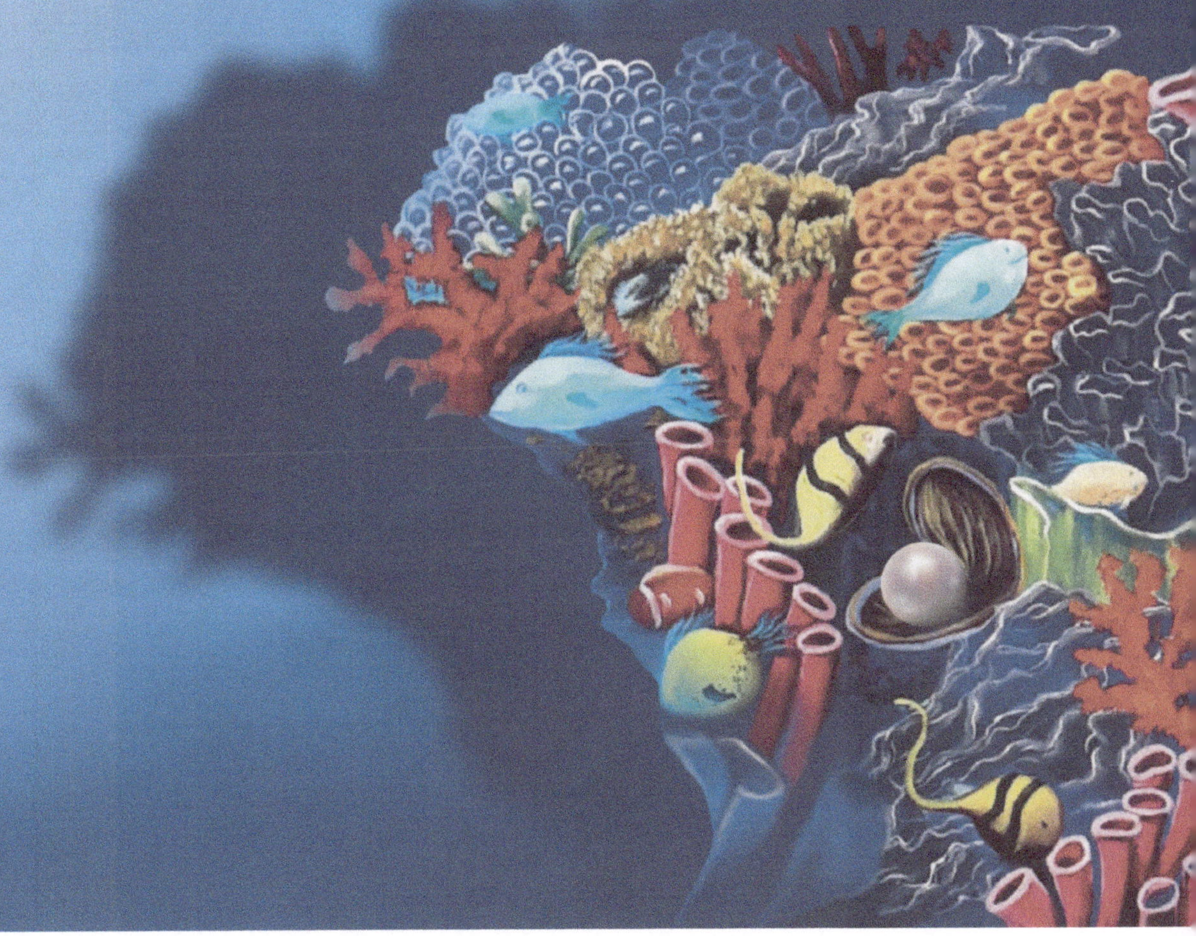

The most playful and fun-loving creatures in the reef are the Dolphins. And the most adventurous among the dolphins is Coty, the newborn bab dolphin, who spends most of her time with her mother learning about th deep blue sea.

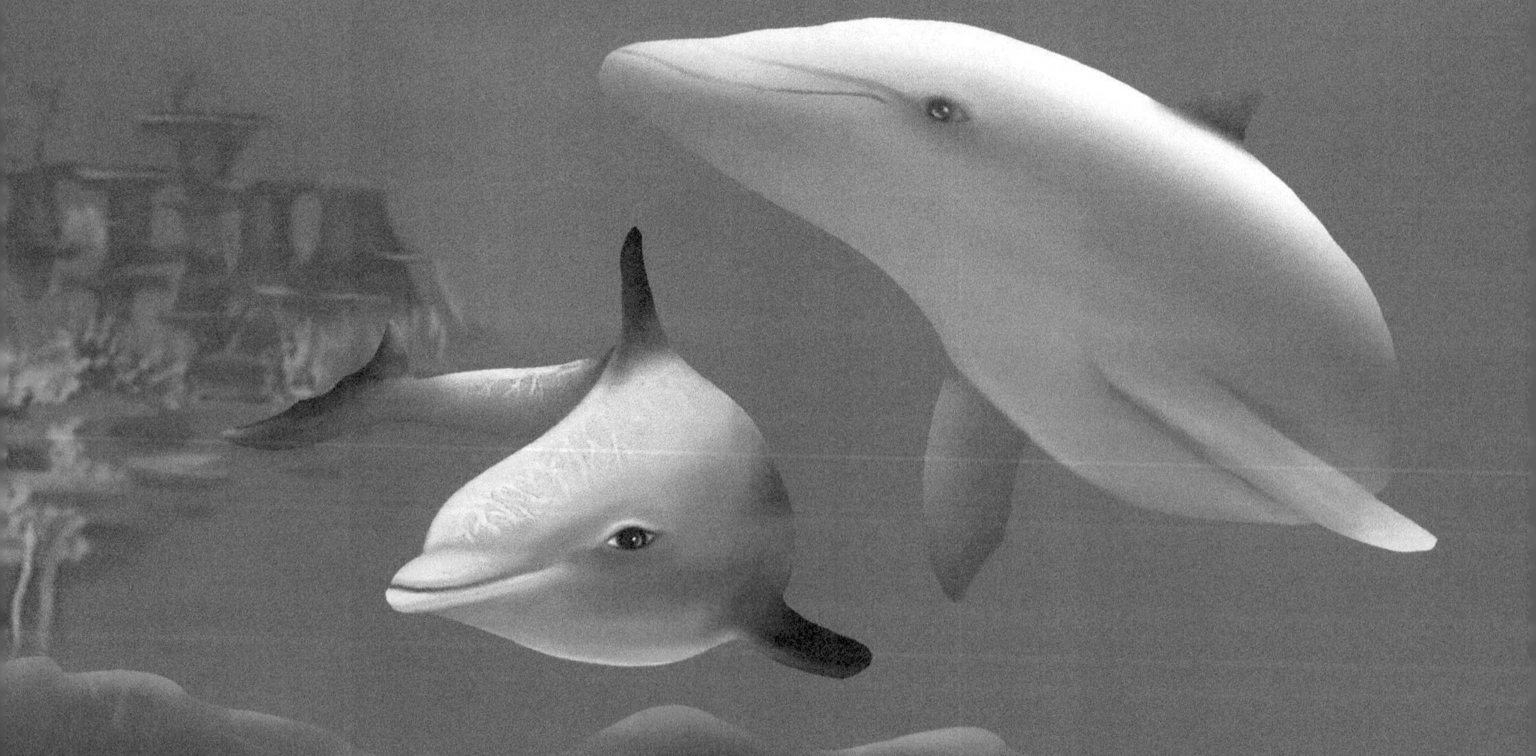

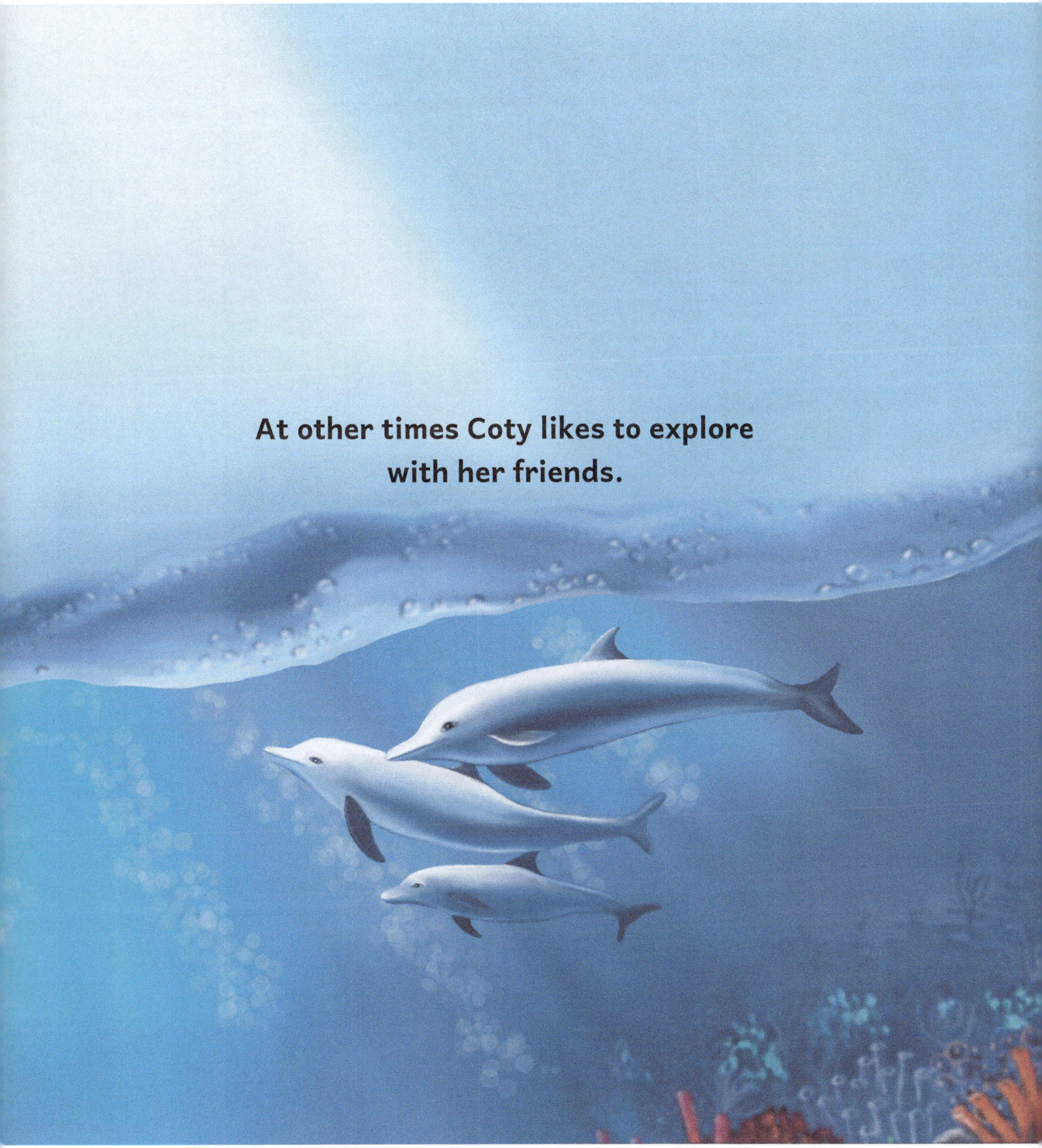
At other times Coty likes to explore
with her friends.

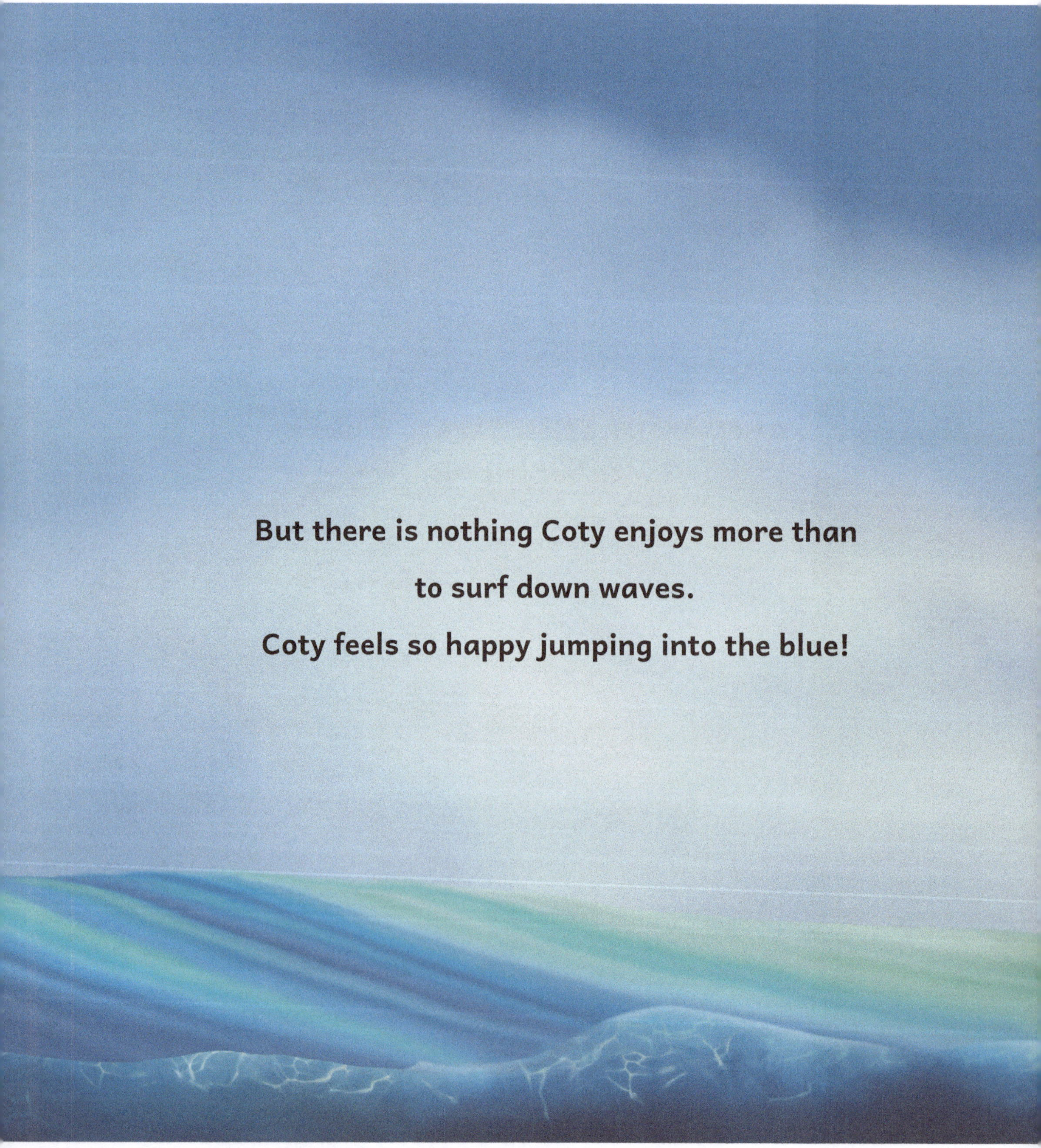

But there is nothing Coty enjoys more than

to surf down waves.

Coty feels so happy jumping into the blue!

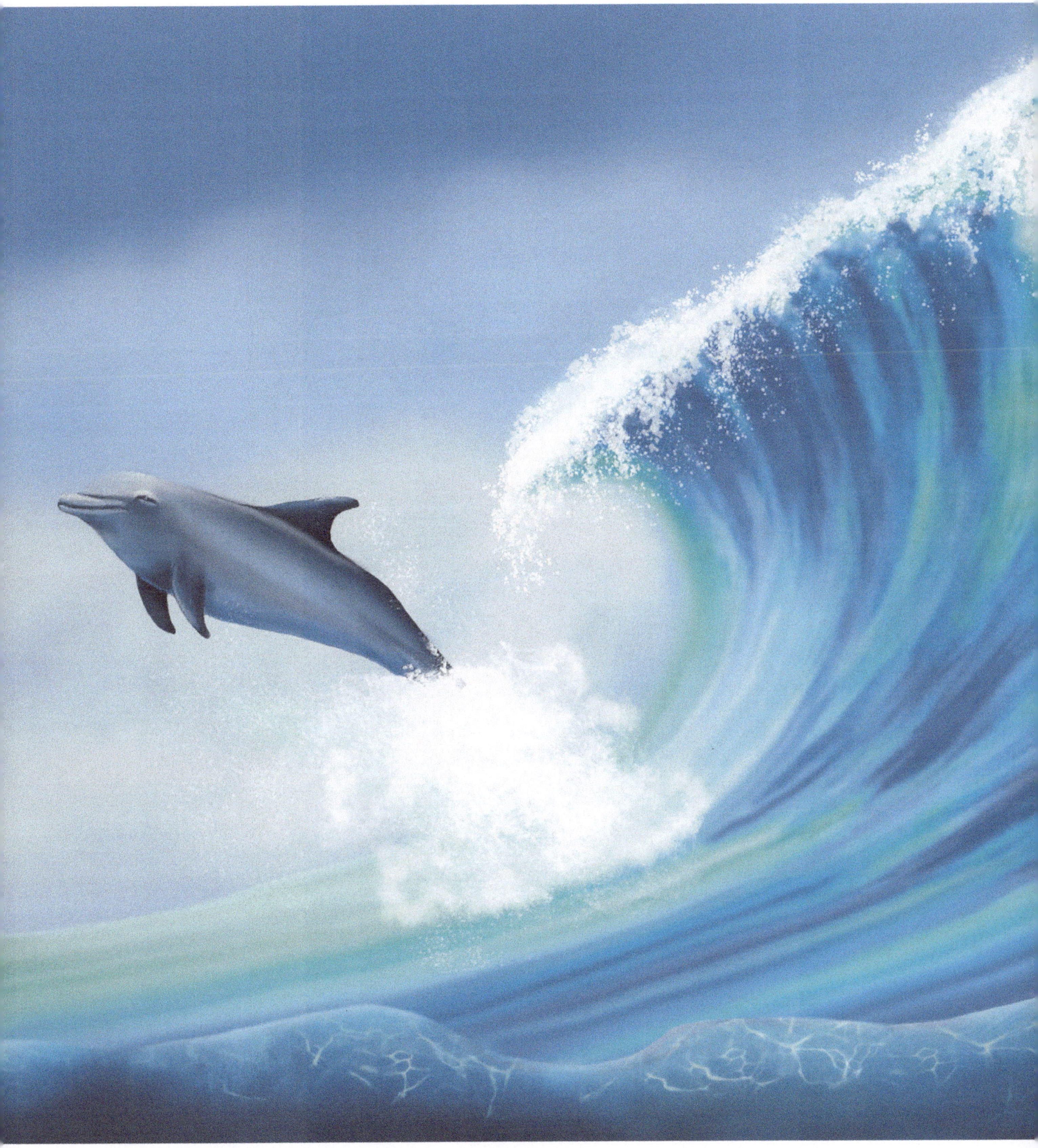

One day, Coty goes out surfing with her friends and almost bumps into a strange being without fins or tail, but with two legs instead.

“It’s a human!” exclaims one of the dolphins.

From behind the waves, they watch in fascination as the human glides along the wave on a surfboard.

Coty finds it hard to believe another creature can enjoy the surf so much and feels an instant connection with the human.

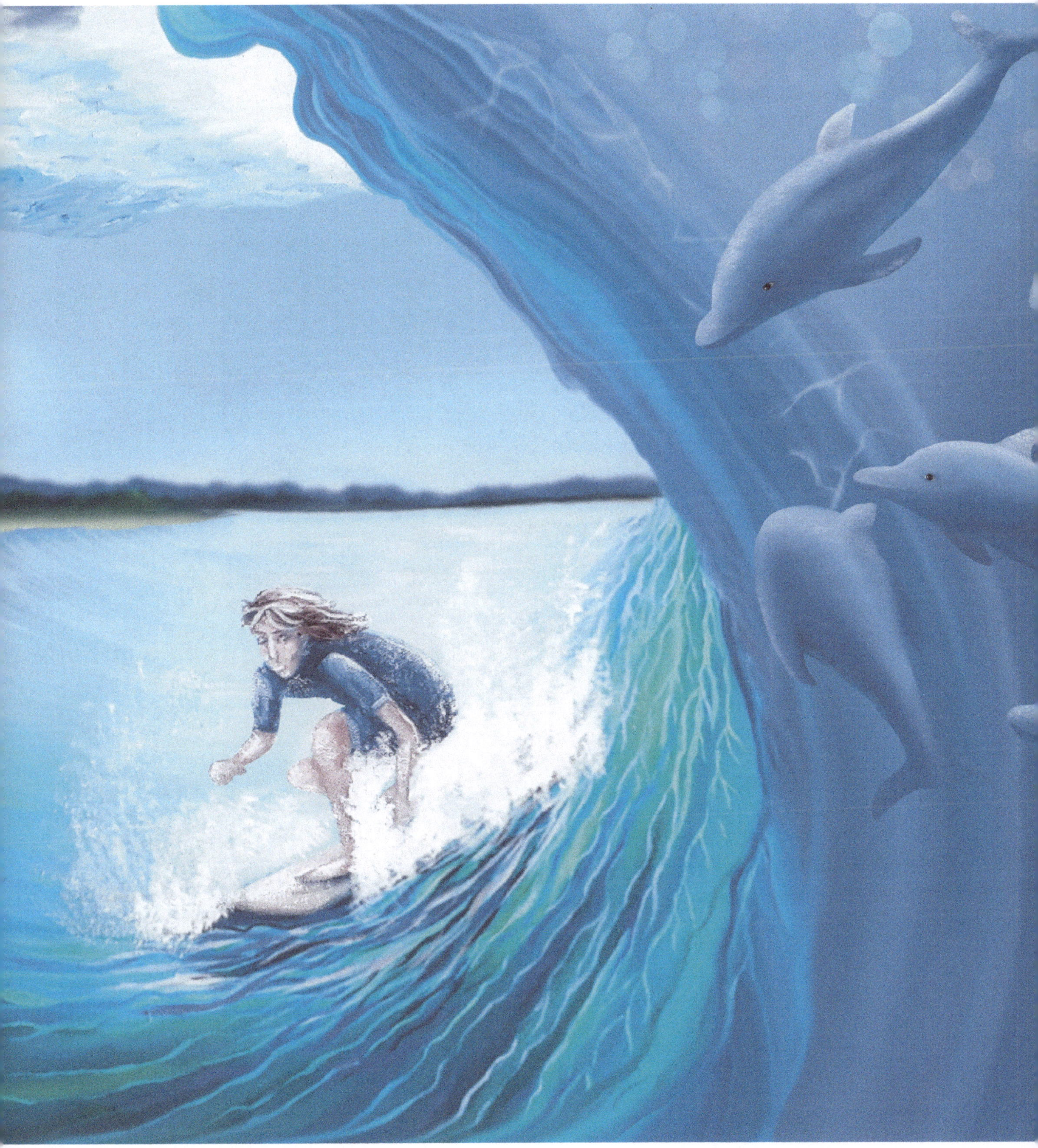

Many days pass...

Then, one day, Coty comes across the surfer once again, this time with a companion looking for something in the deep sea. Curious and wanting to make friends, Coty decides to follow them.

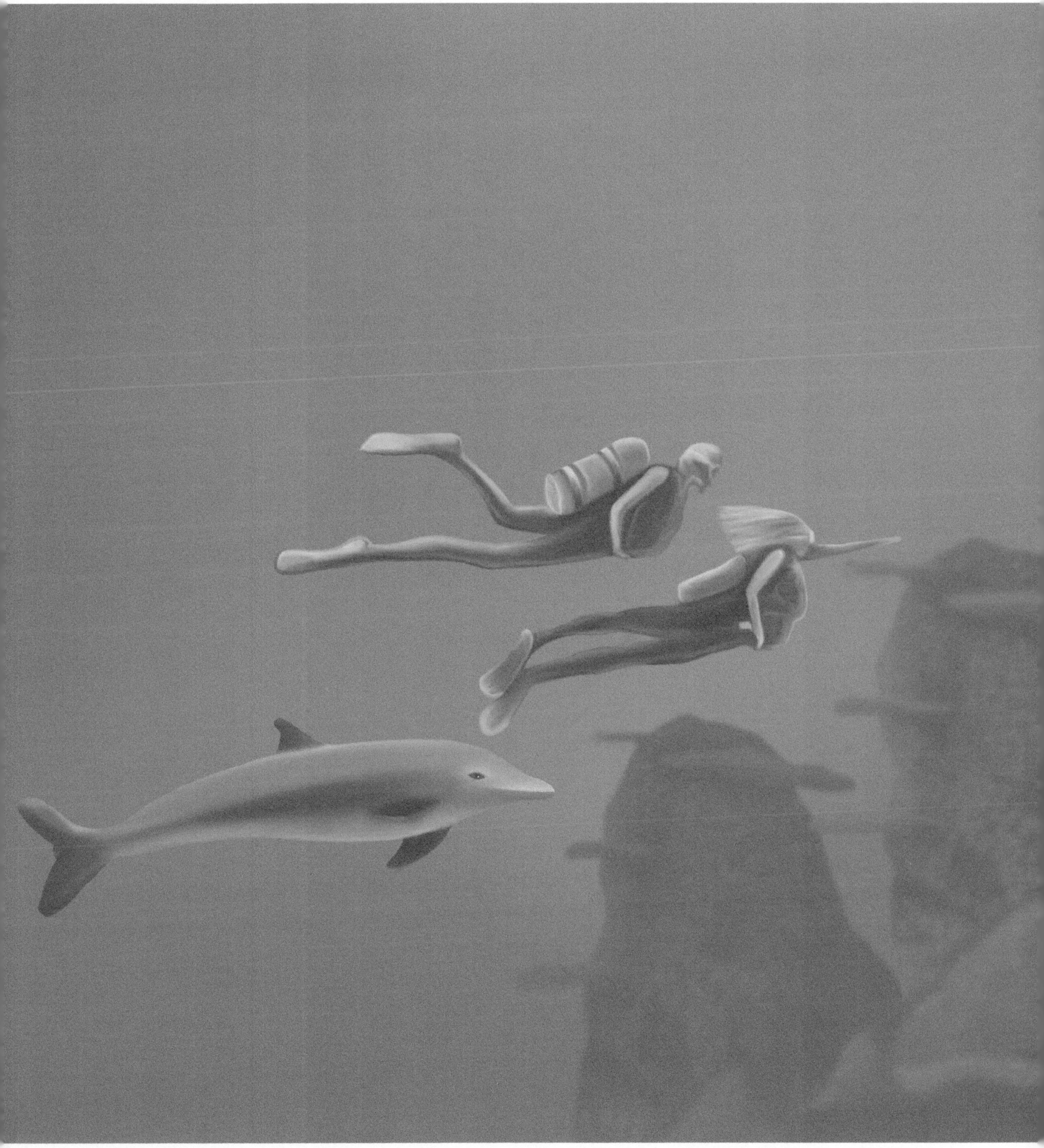

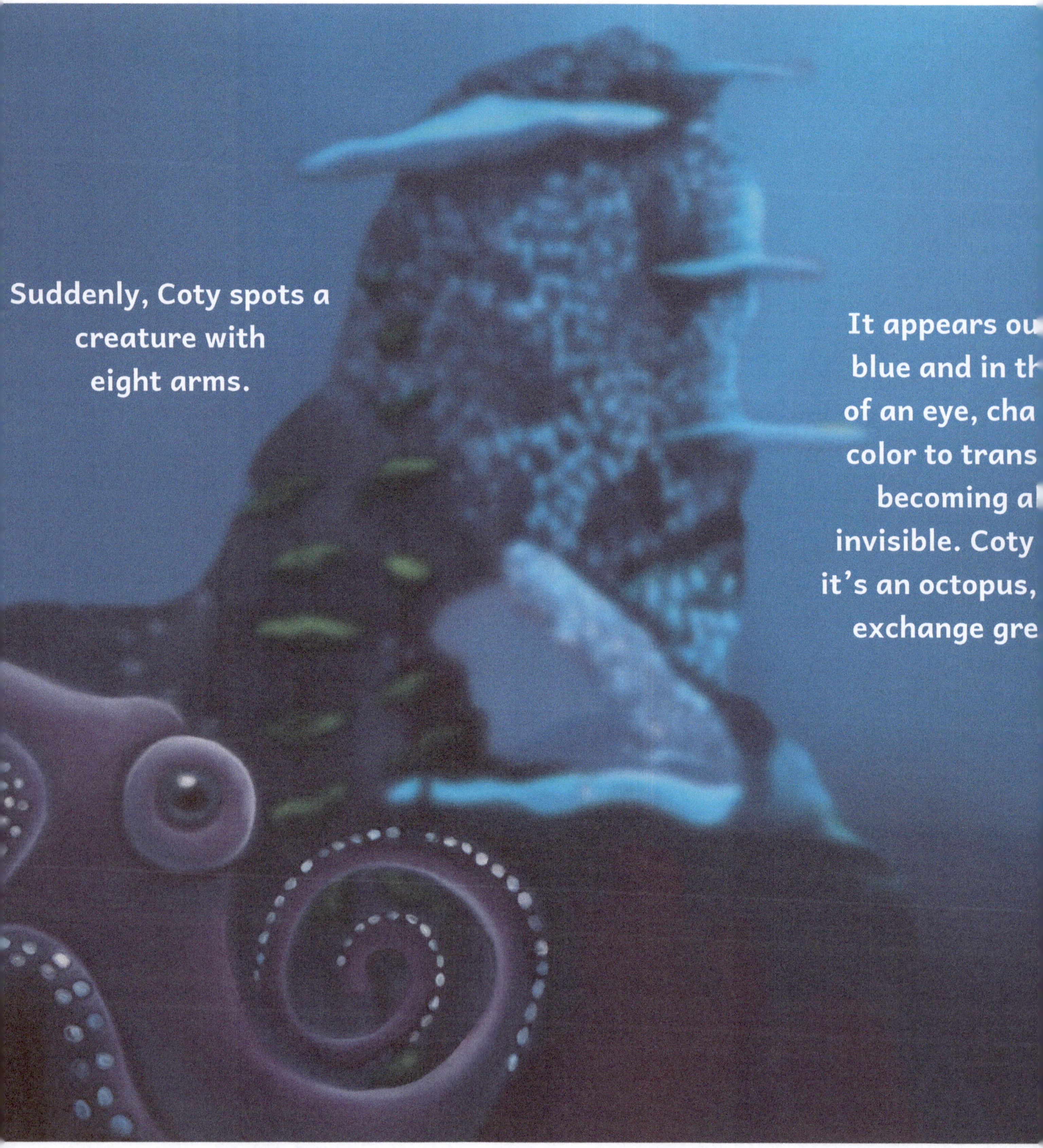

Suddenly, Coty spots a
creature with
eight arms.

It appears ou
blue and in th
of an eye, cha
color to trans
becoming a
invisible. Coty
it's an octopus,
exchange gre

“It’s amazing how you can hide in plain sight, Mr. Octopus!”, Coty praises.

“That’s not all”, the octopus replies,

“I have three hearts with blue blood

and I can multi-task which means I can do many things at the same time”.

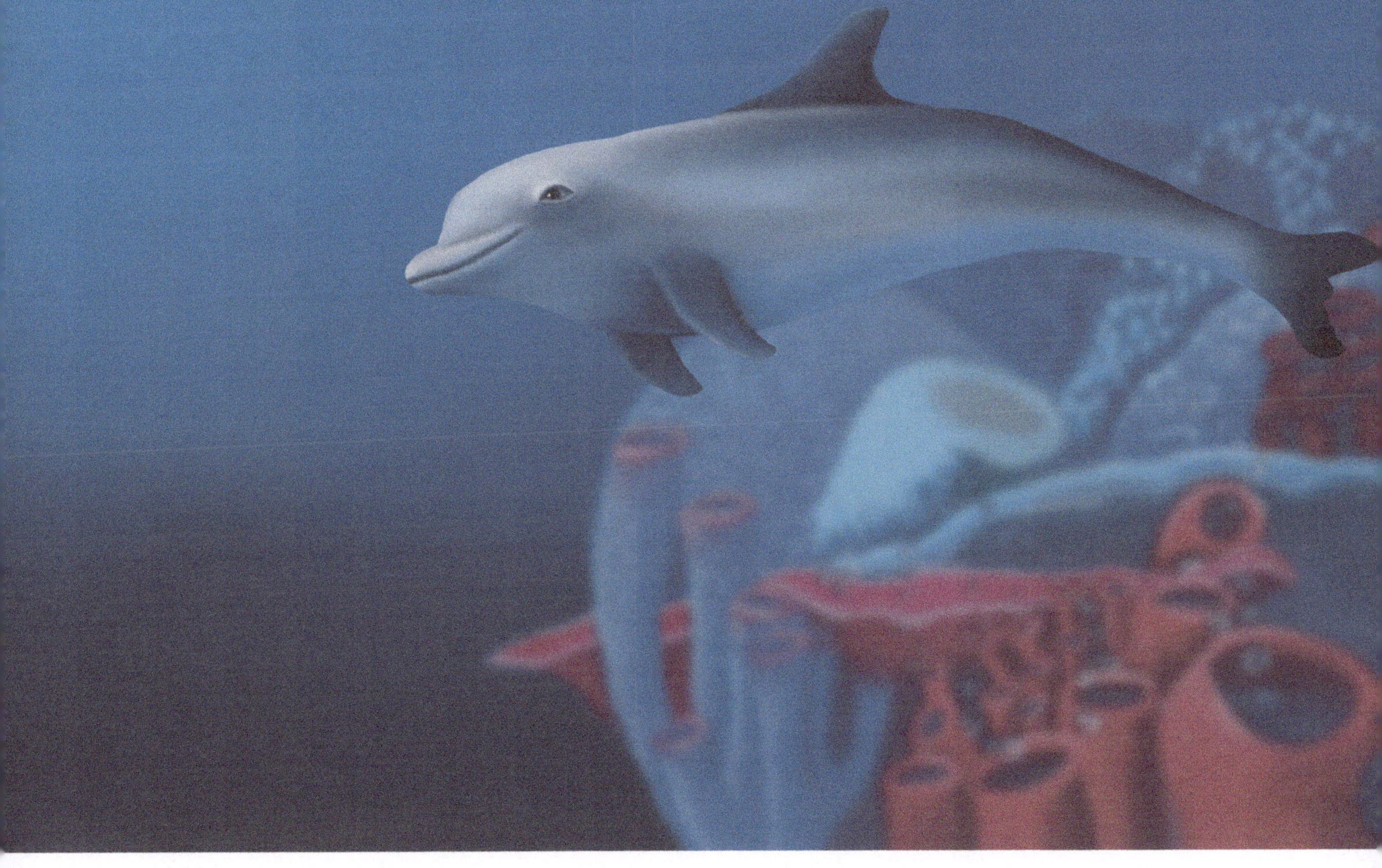

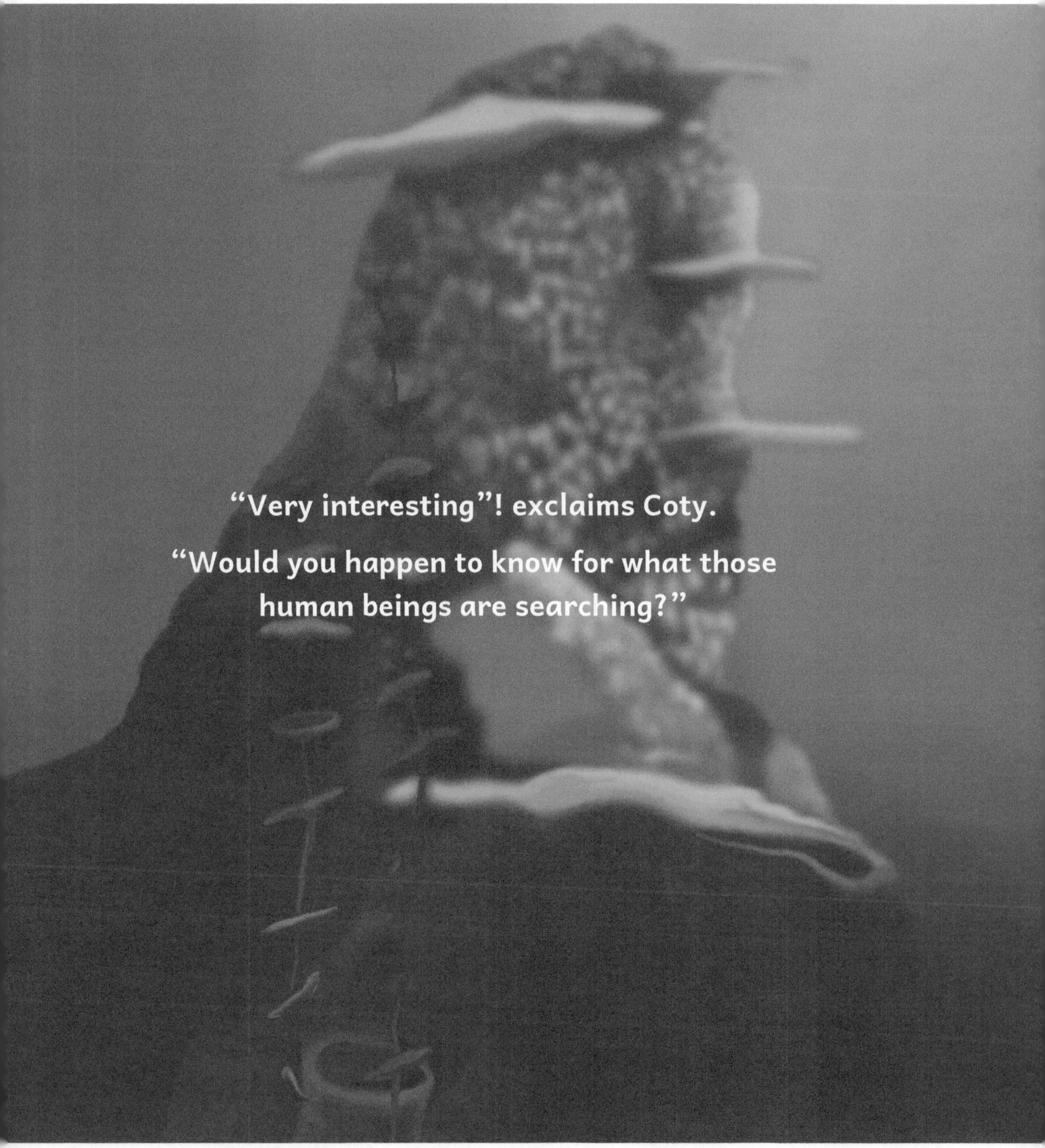

"Very interesting"! exclaims Coty.

"Would you happen to know for what those human beings are searching?"

ing a sea turtle approaching, the octopus replies,
Mrs.Tortuga. She is more than a hundred years old
actually met many humans on her visits to the beach".

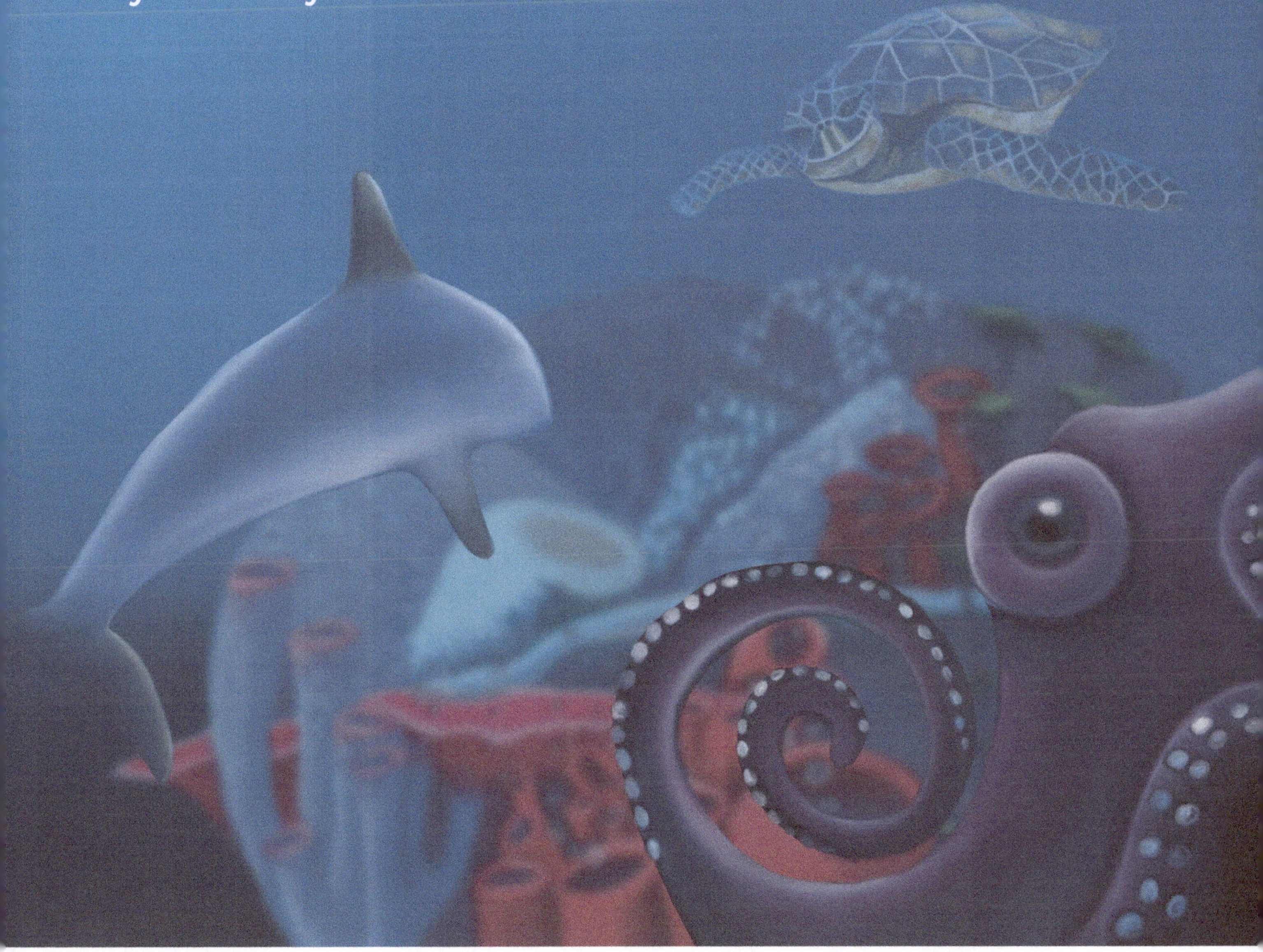

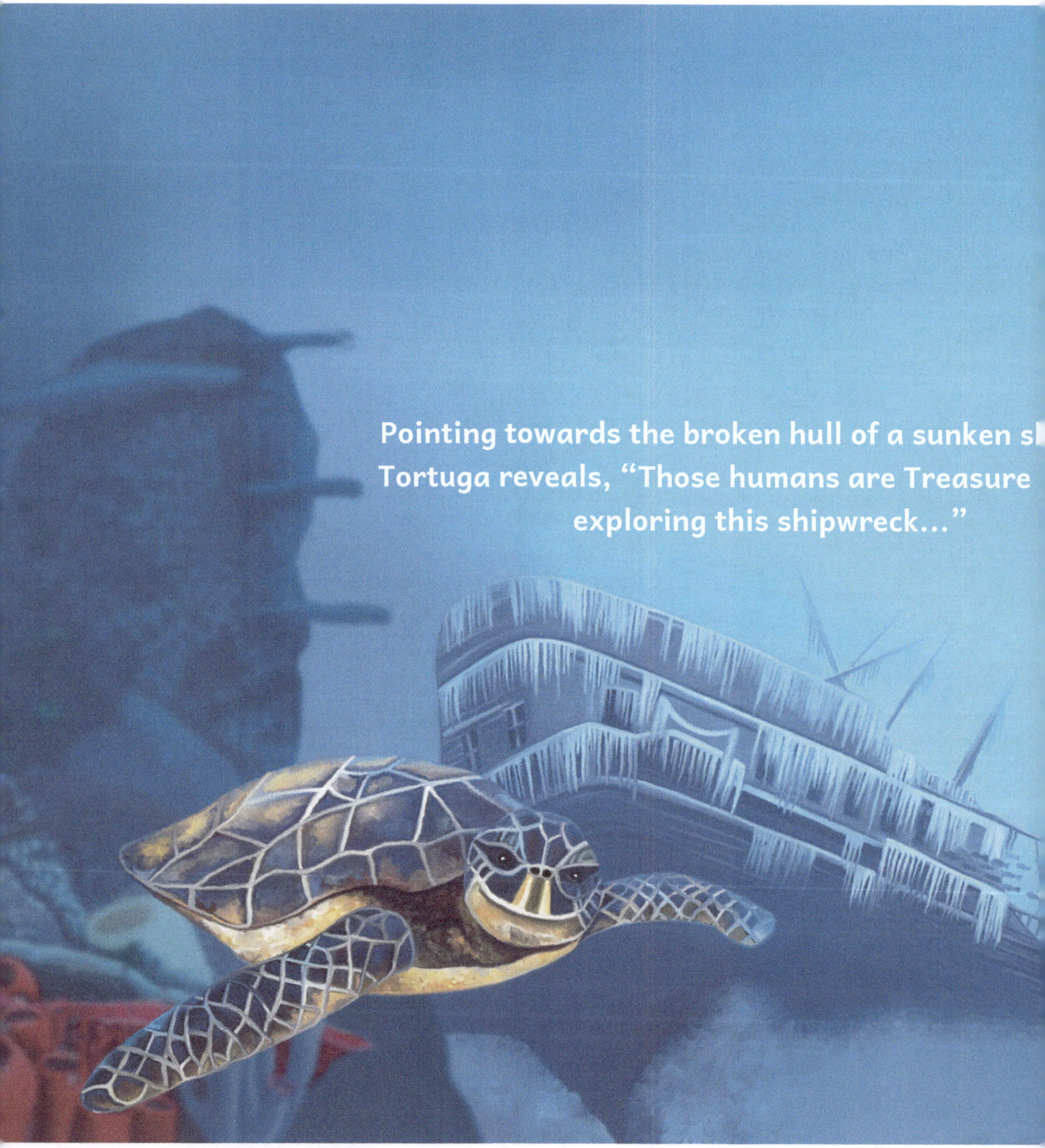

Pointing towards the broken hull of a sunken sh
Tortuga reveals, "Those humans are Treasure
exploring this shipwreck..."

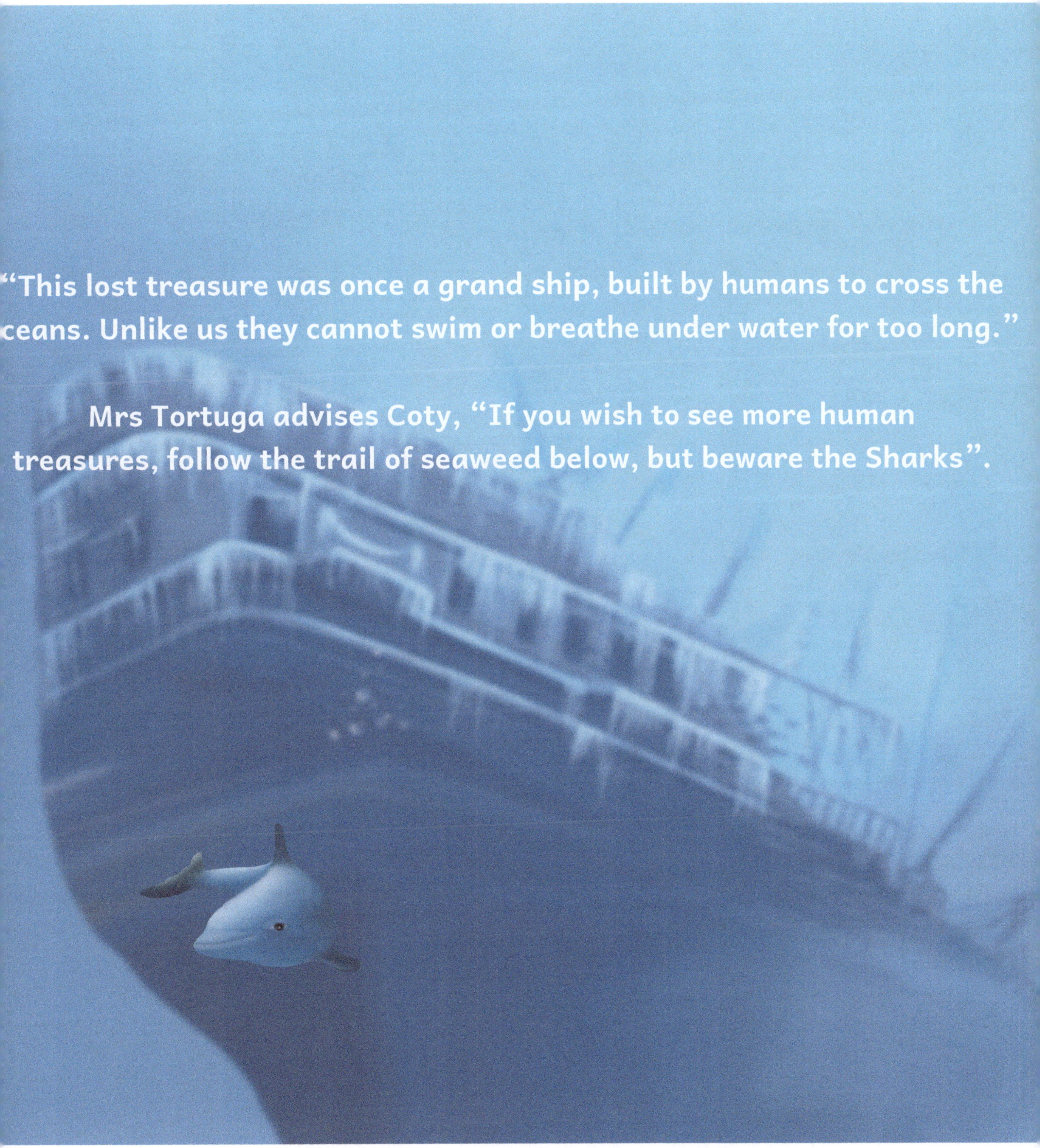

“This lost treasure was once a grand ship, built by humans to cross the ceans. Unlike us they cannot swim or breathe under water for too long.”

Mrs Tortuga advises Coty, “If you wish to see more human treasures, follow the trail of seaweed below, but beware the Sharks”.

Thanking, Mrs. Tortuga, Coty continues down the seaweed path.

She has only heard her mother speak of sharks
but never actually encountered one,
and so is not scared...

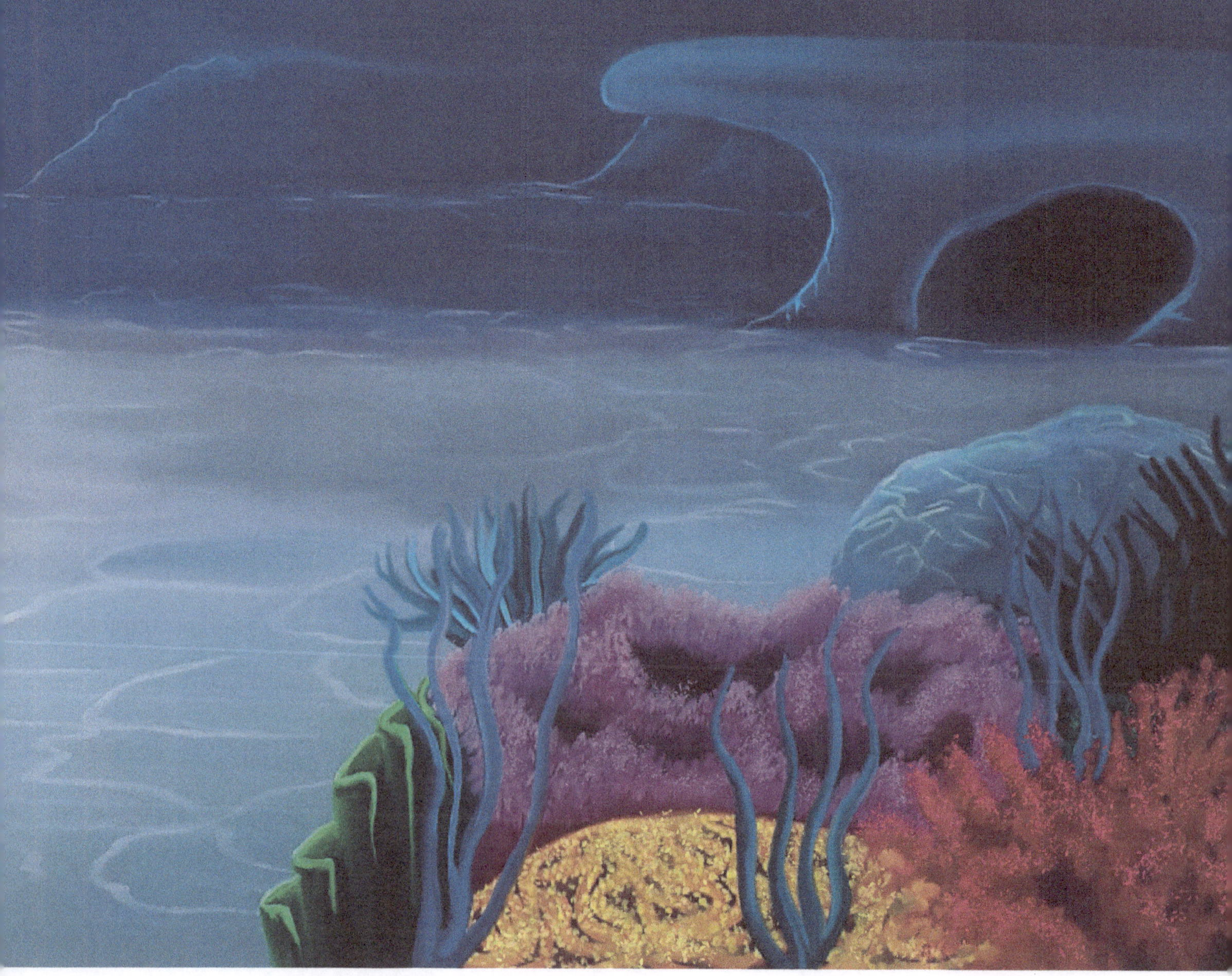

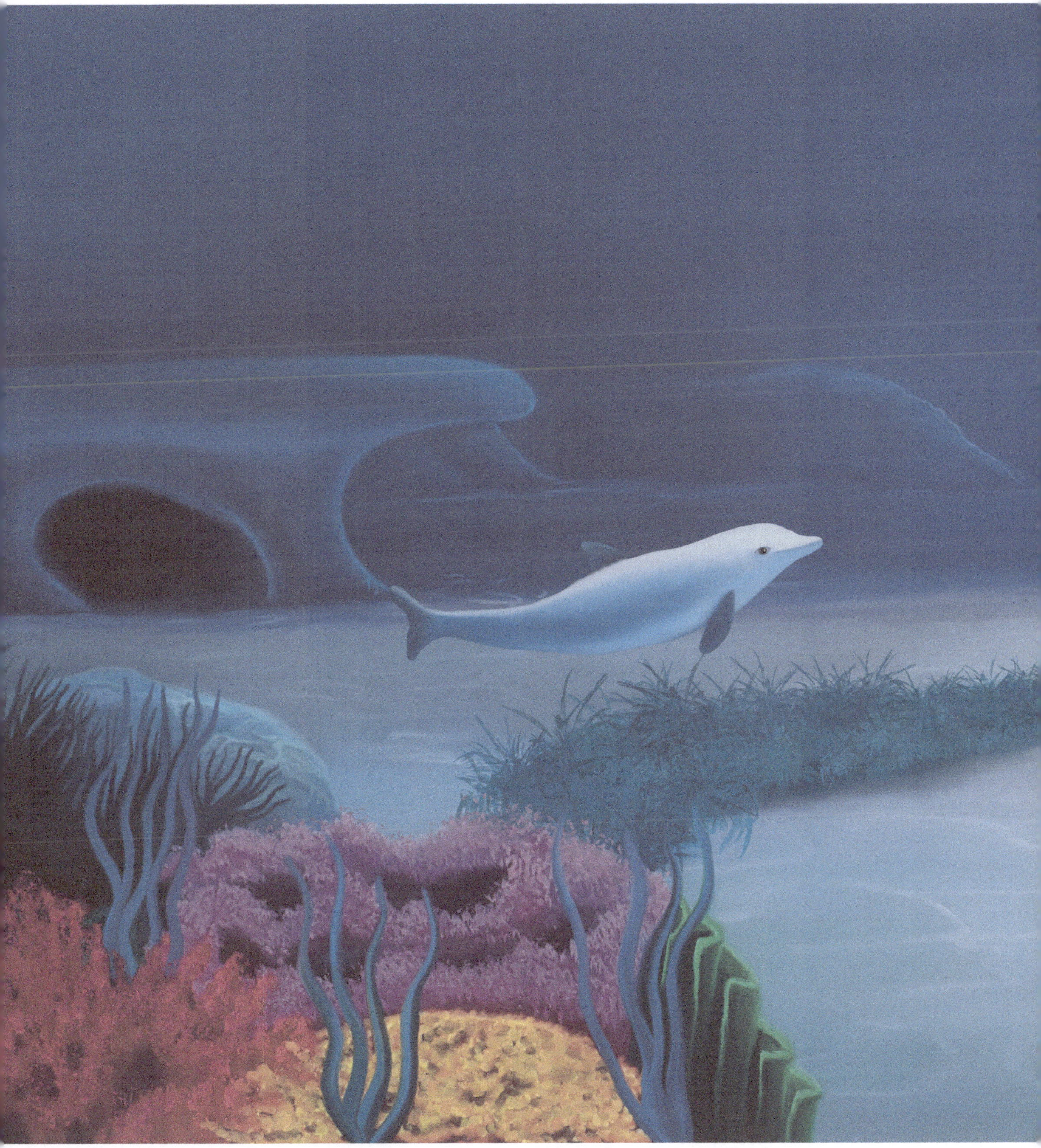

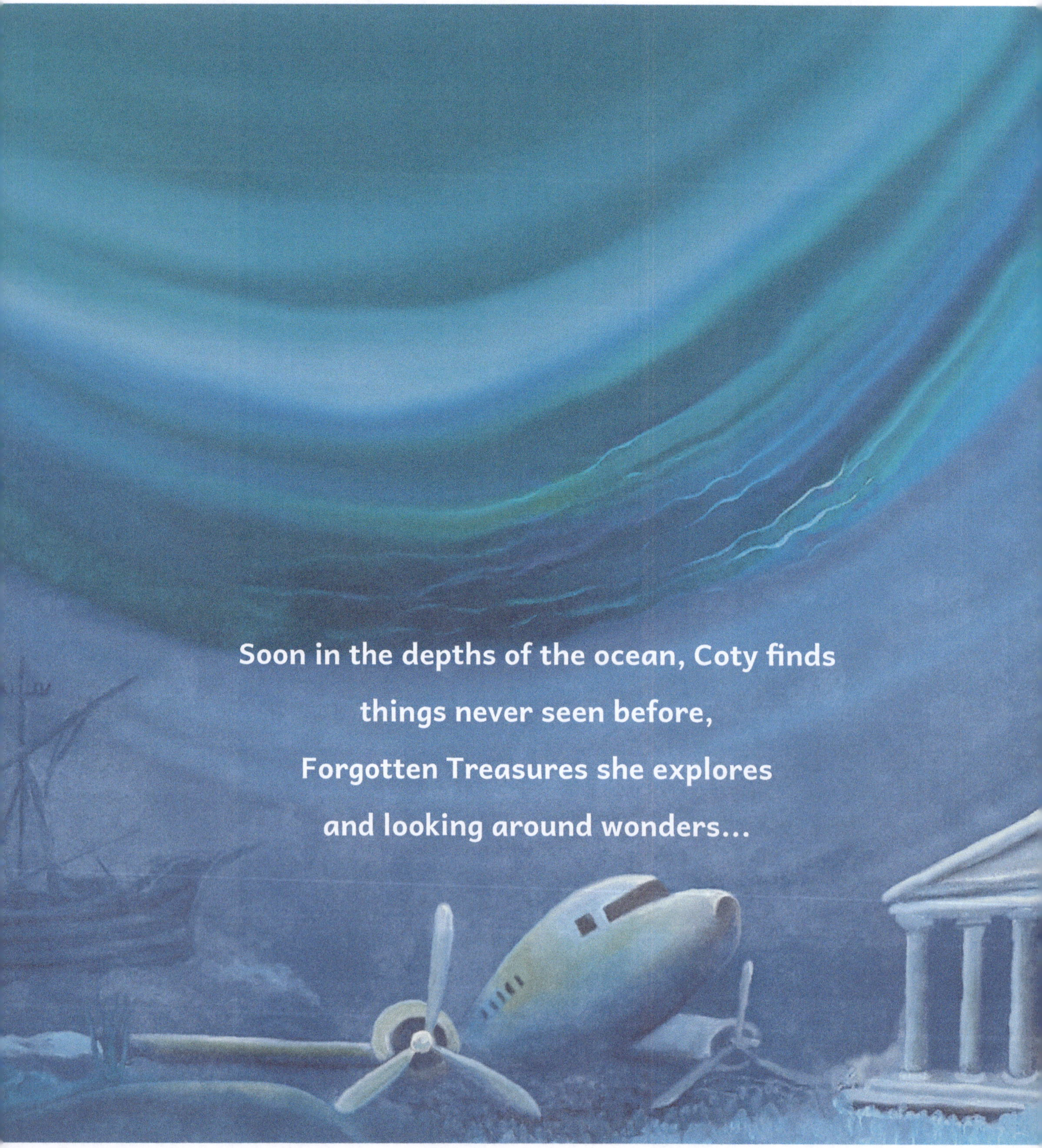

Soon in the depths of the ocean, Coty finds
things never seen before,
Forgotten Treasures she explores
and looking around wonders...

Strange objects lost at sea, that humans come from time to time to seek”.

ese objects worth a lot must be, but which treasures are valuable for me?”

Finally tired and hungry, Coty decides to return home.

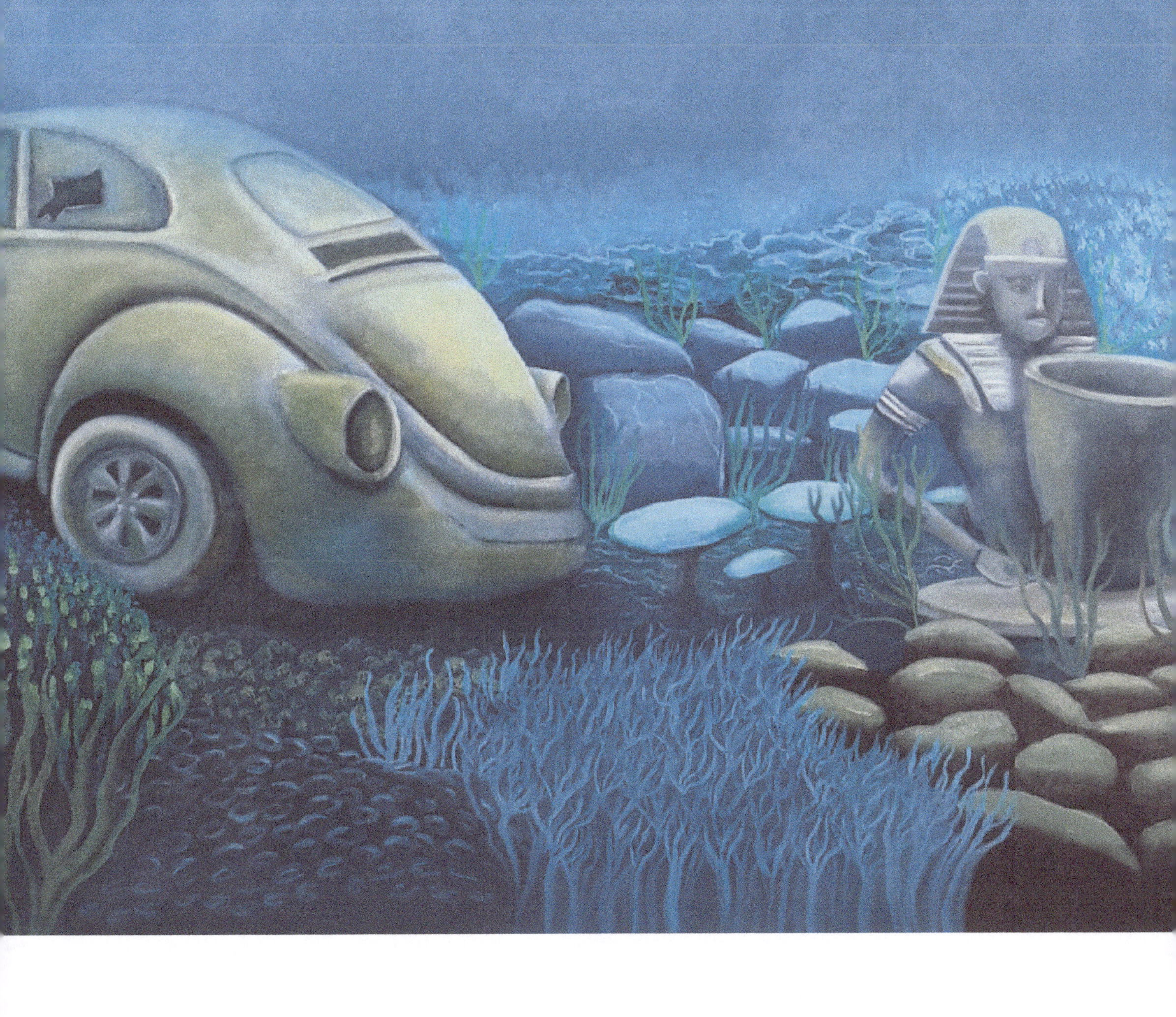

On her way home Coty meets

a shoal of fish frozen in fear,

trying to warn her but unable to get the words out.

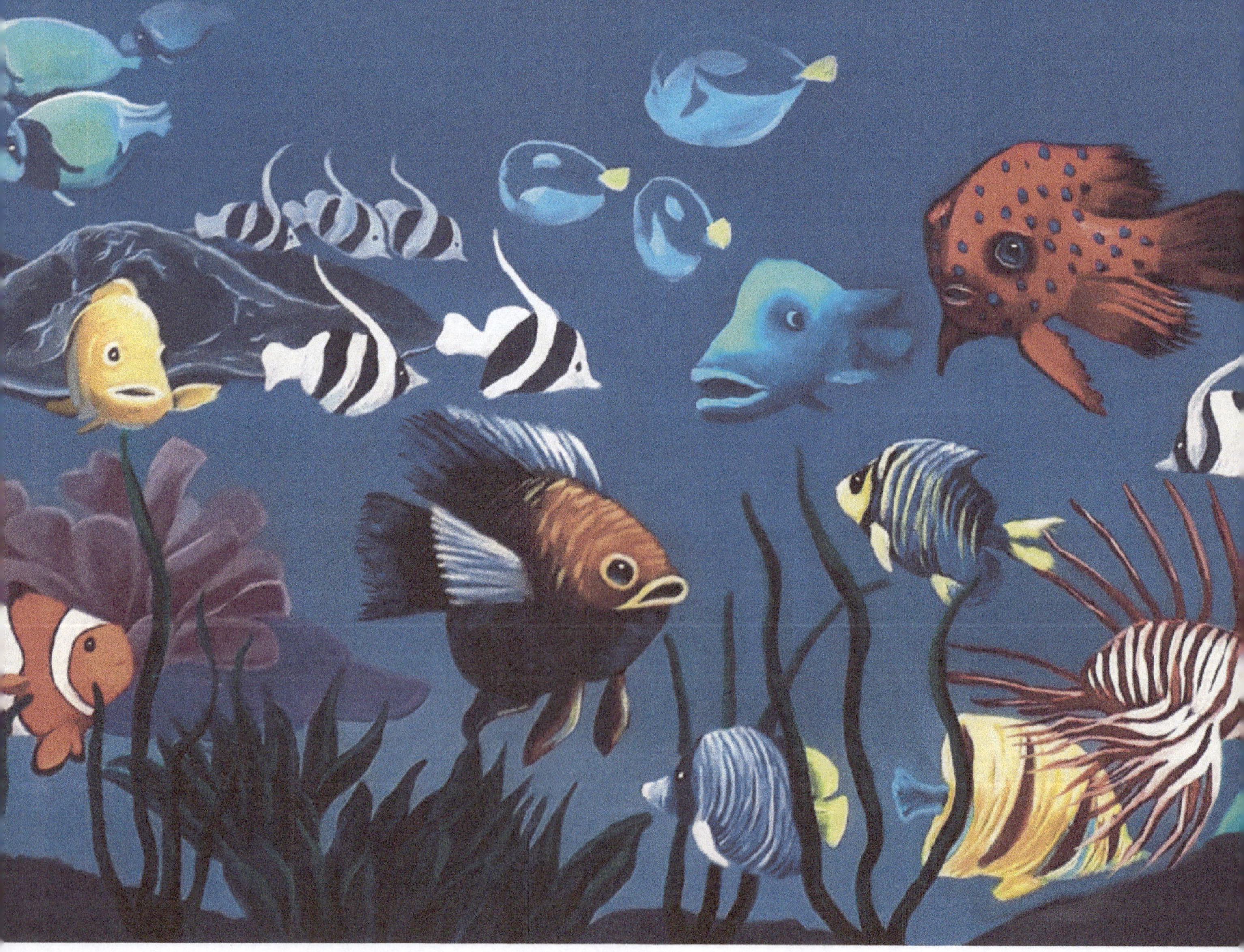

"Sharks, watch out!" a fish at last exclaims

and leaving Coty alone, they all flee.

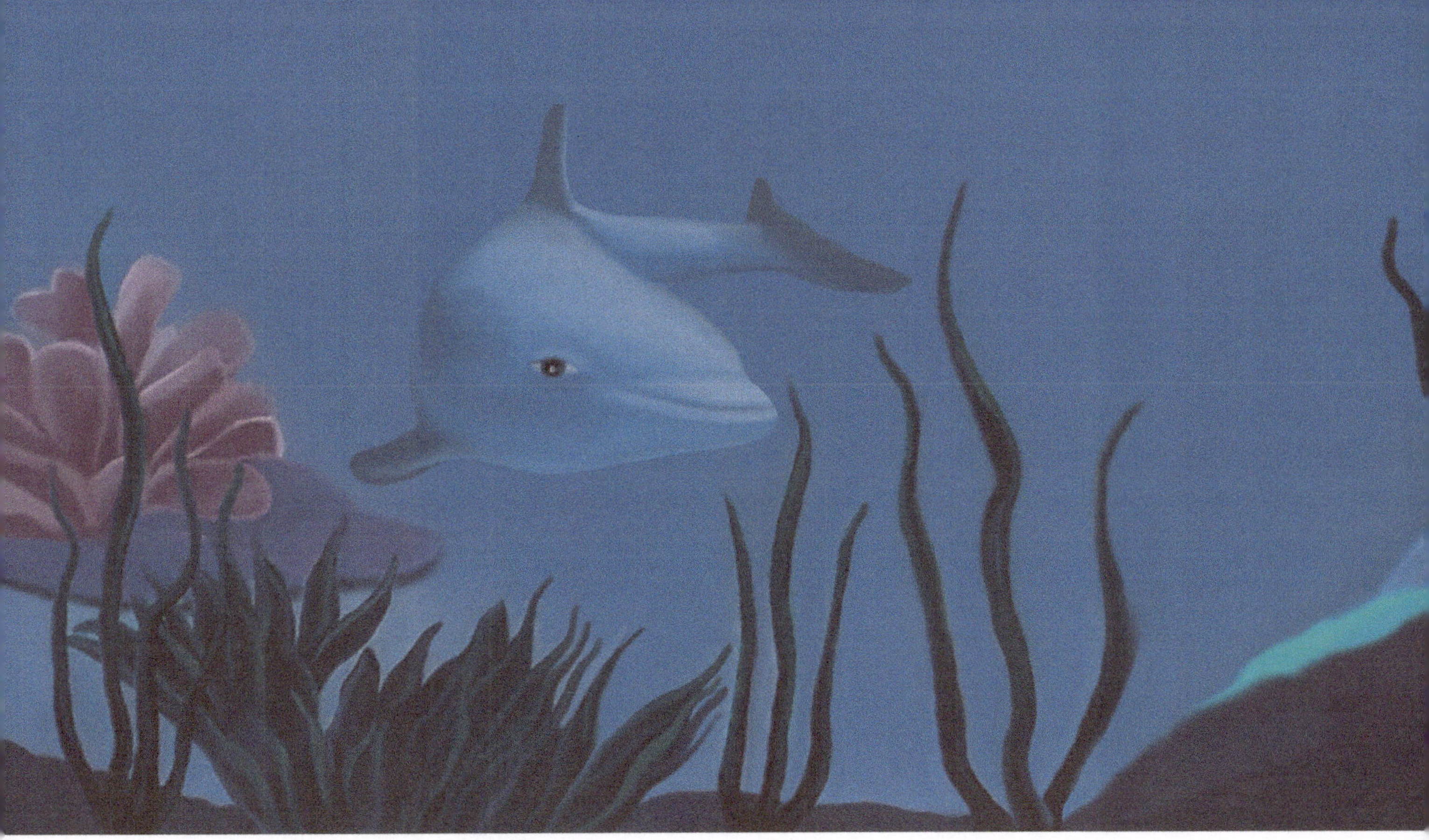

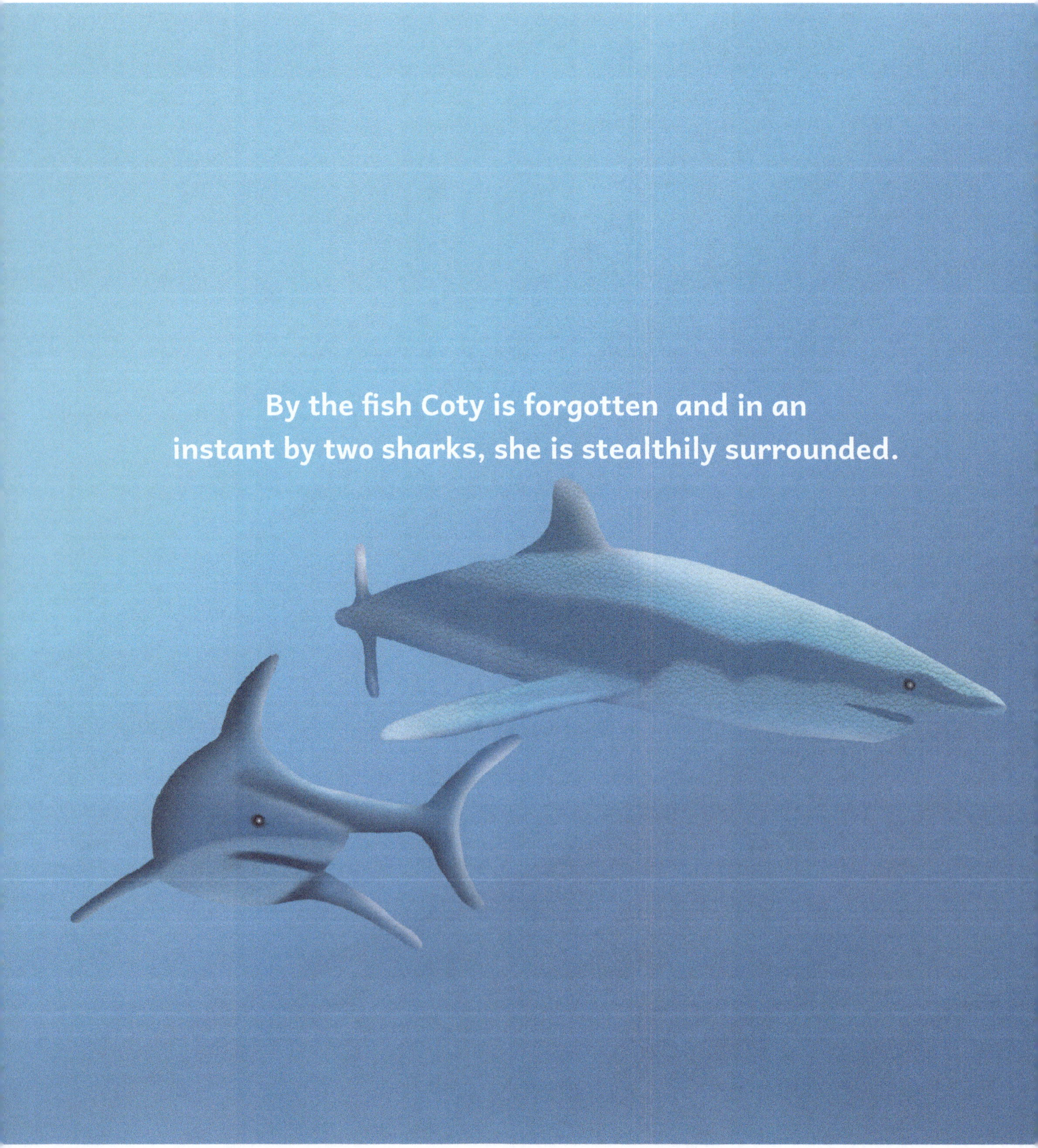

By the fish Coty is forgotten and in an
instant by two sharks, she is stealthily surrounded.

Coty, paralyzed with fear,

hears one of them whisper,

"For us you will be a very tasty lunch,
so small and easy to munch."

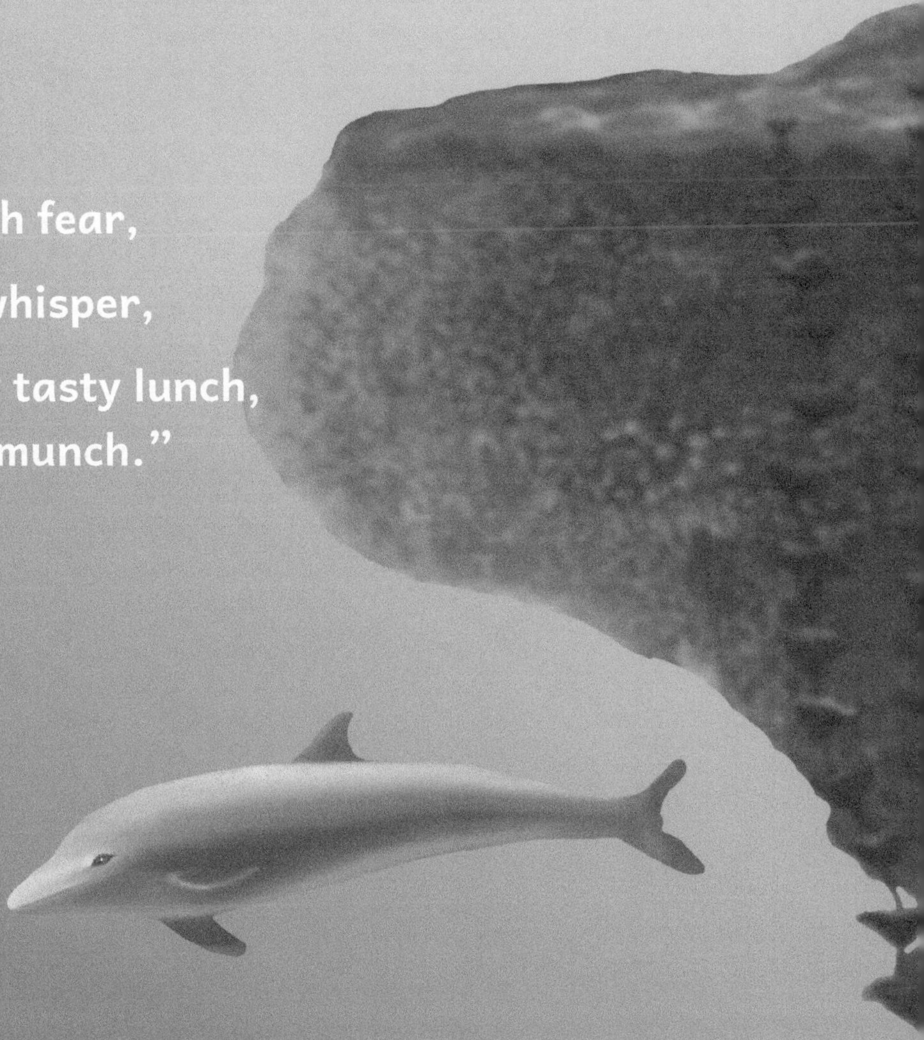

Just then, she hears a sound,

and the sharks flee in terror.

Coty wonders what it is that just saved her.

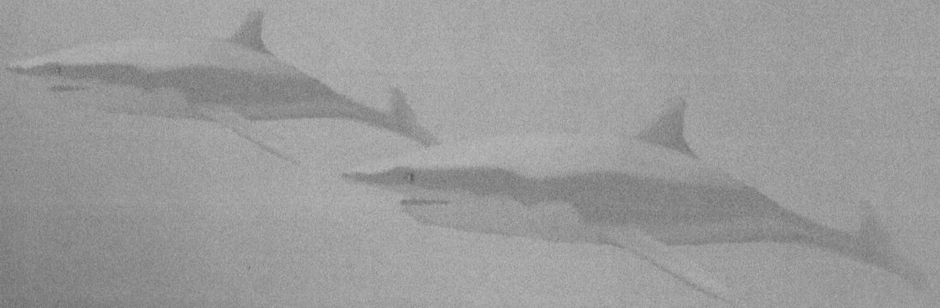

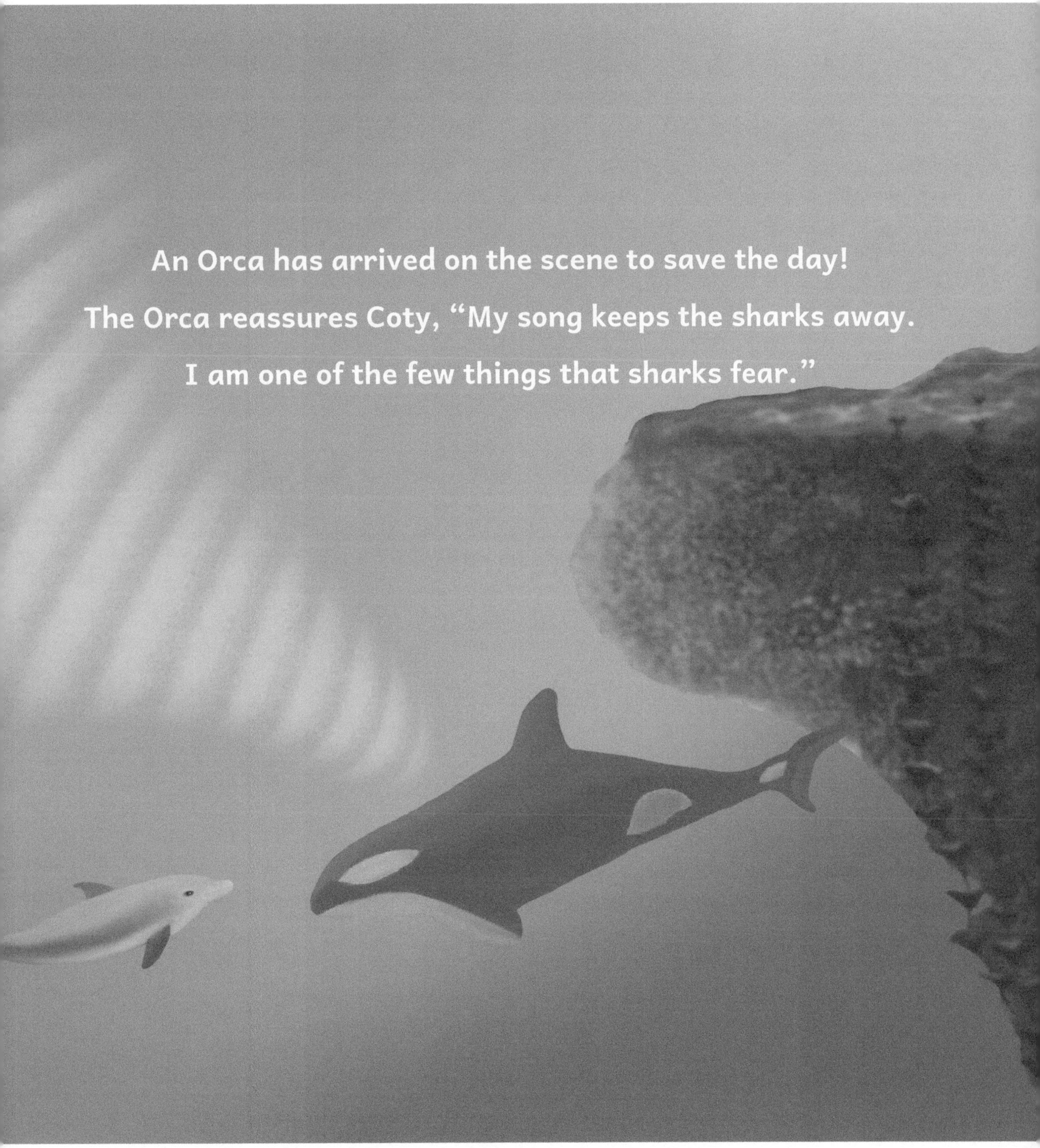

An Orca has arrived on the scene to save the day!

The Orca reassures Coty, "My song keeps the sharks away.

I am one of the few things that sharks fear."

Vithout further ado, the Orca invites Coty to a celebration with other orc

Together they leap out of the sea and

Coty witnesses a fantastic light shining in the sky like no other.

"Celebrating the arrival of the amazing light we are.

Aurora borealis or northern lights, the humans call it", explains the Orc

"Come join us, Coty
we are not the only ones celebrating."

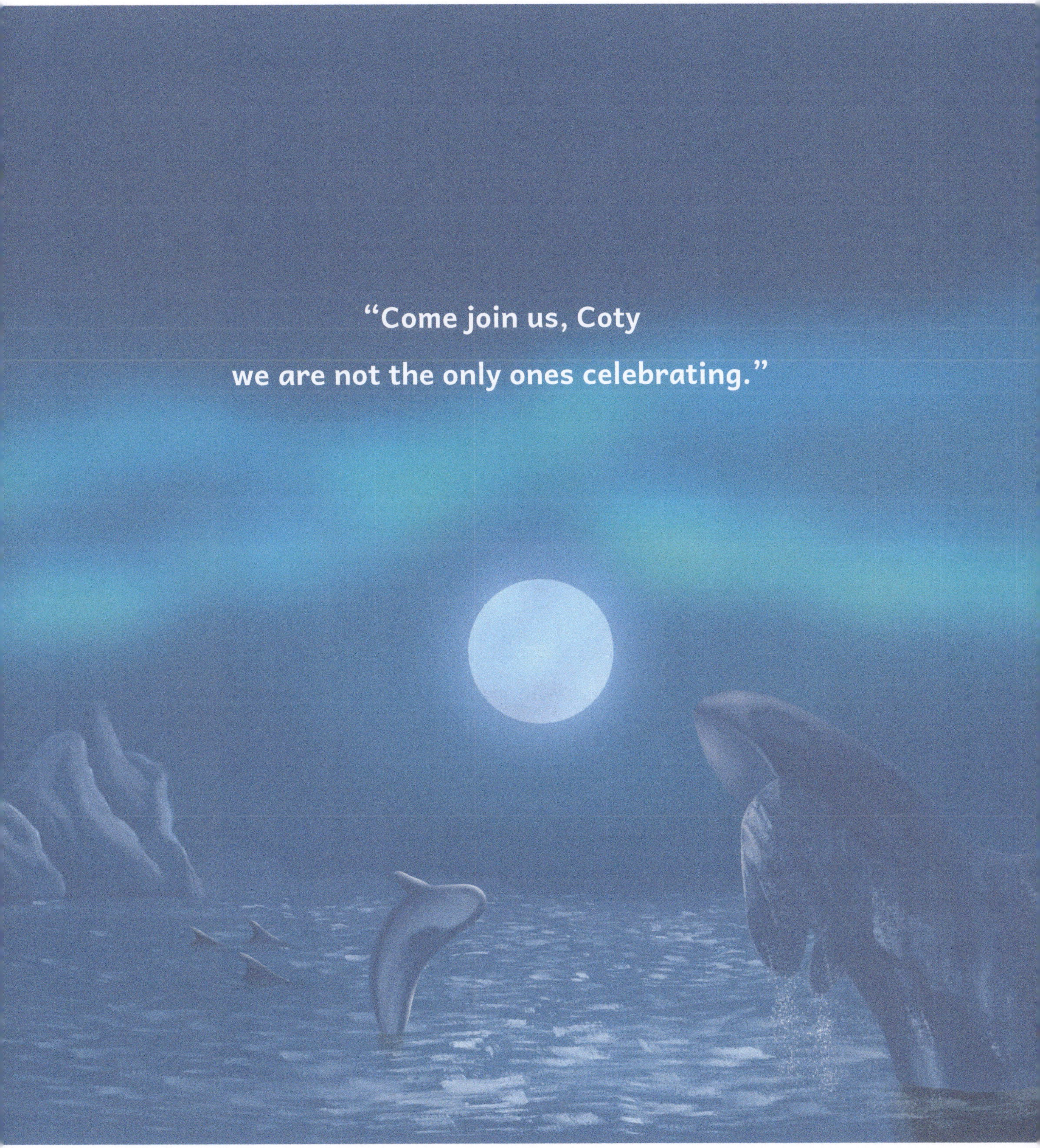

Diving into the sea again, Coty and the orcas are enchanted by glowing creatures.

"Coty, meet the jellyfish. They shine with their own light, and light up the sea!", explains the Orca.

Happy with her adventures of the day, Coty finally feels it is time to say goodbye and head home.

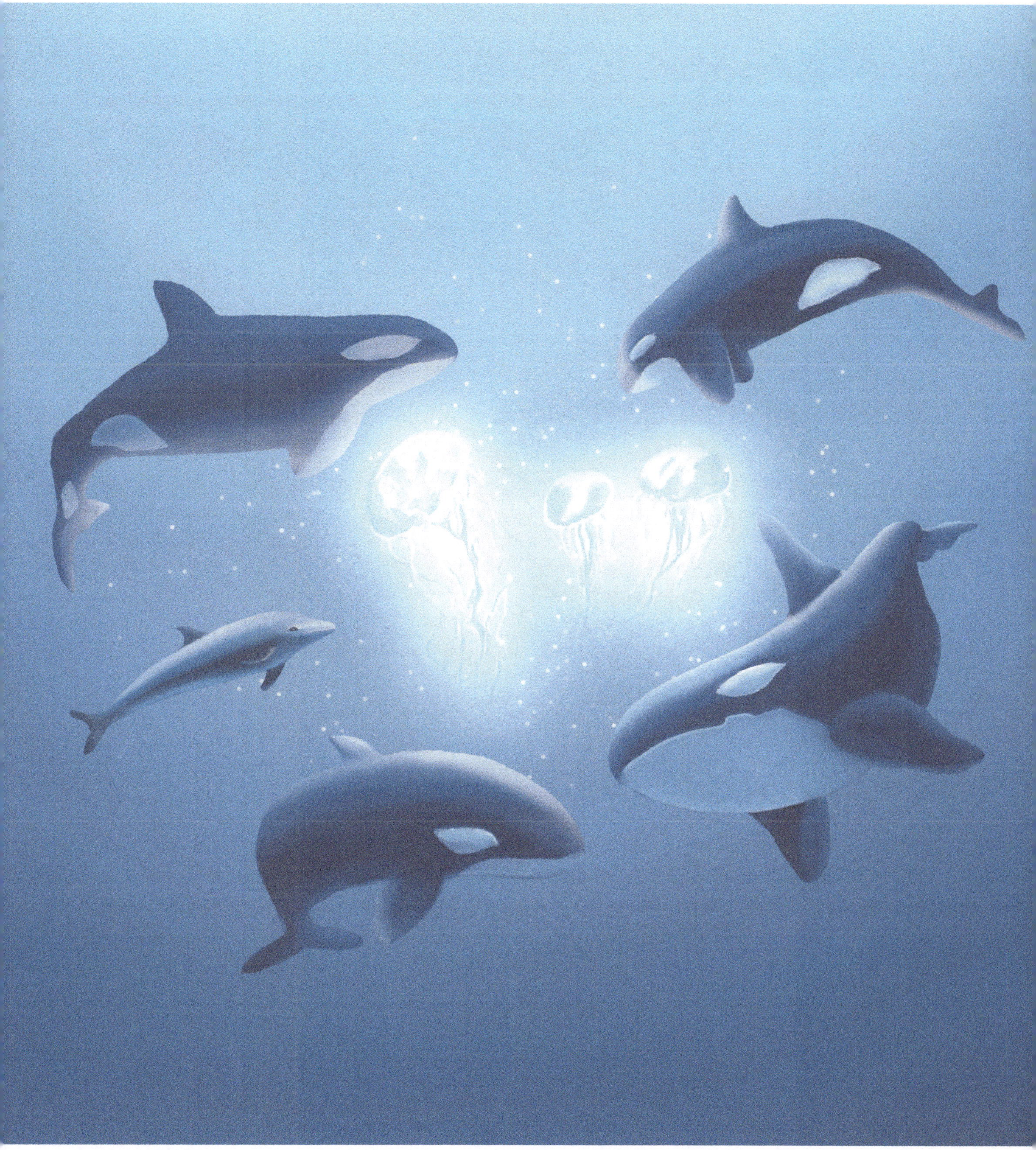

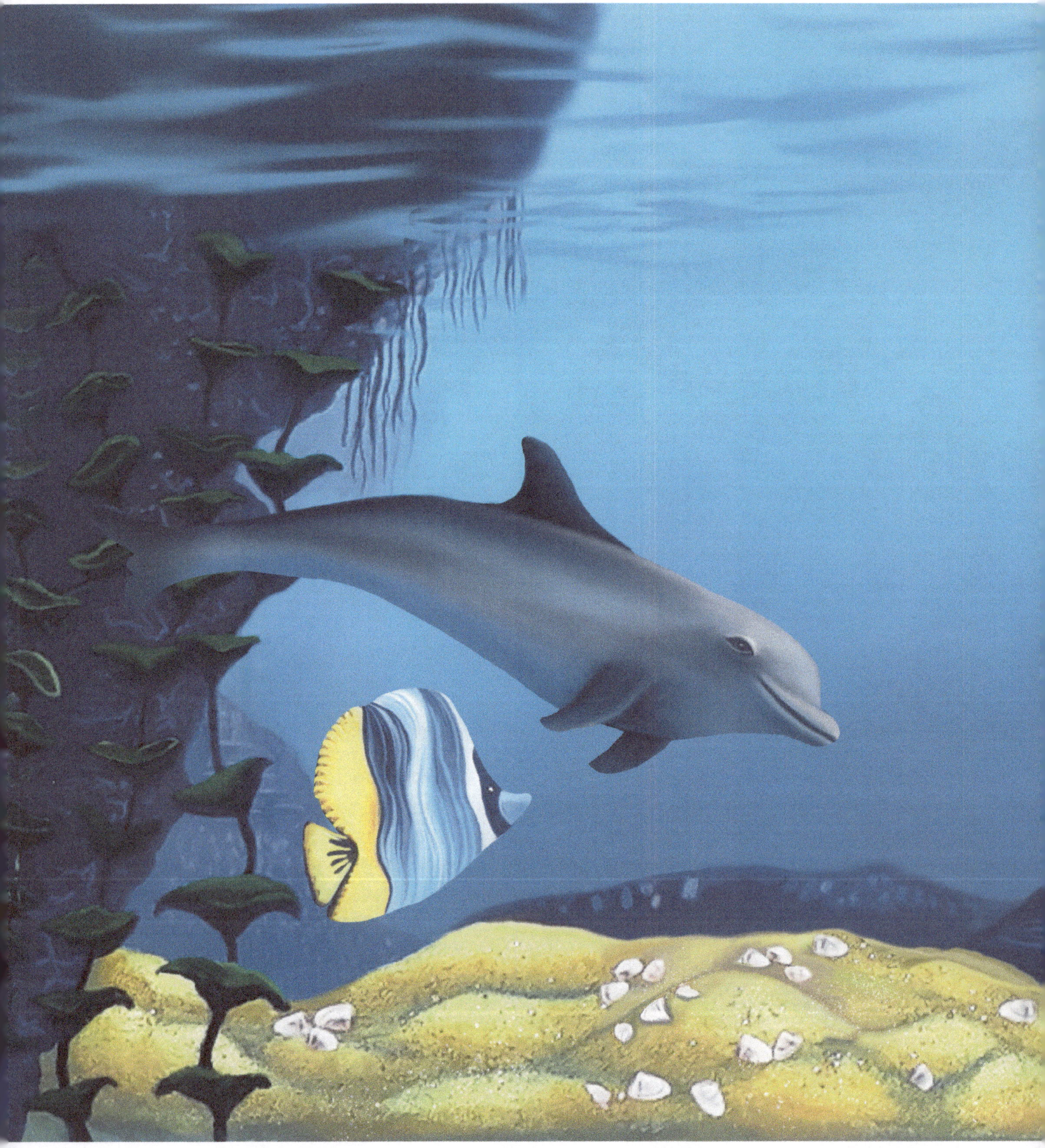

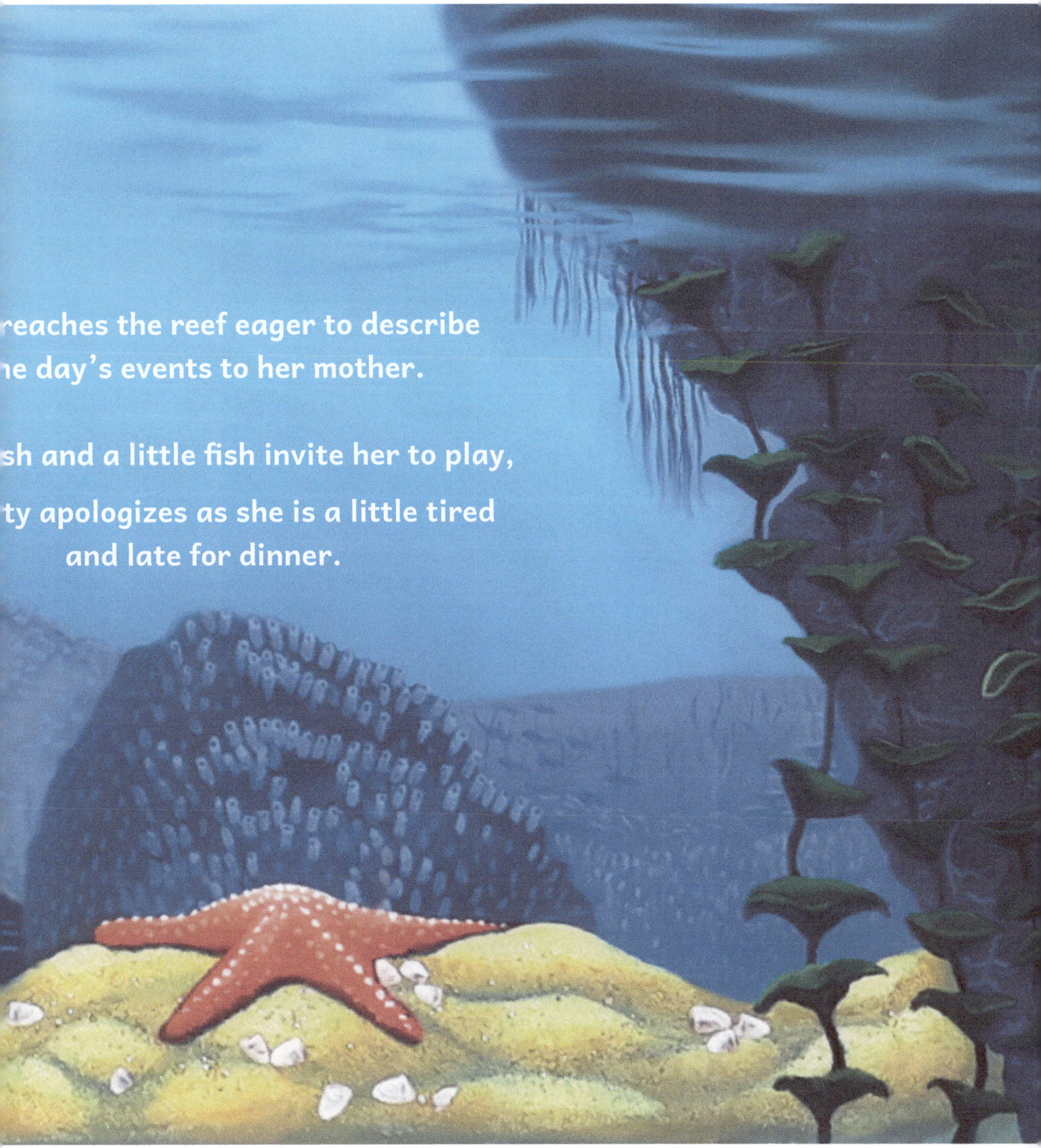

reaches the reef eager to describe
ne day's events to her mother.

sh and *a* little fish invite her to play,

ty *a*pologizes *a*s she is *a* little tired
and late for dinner.

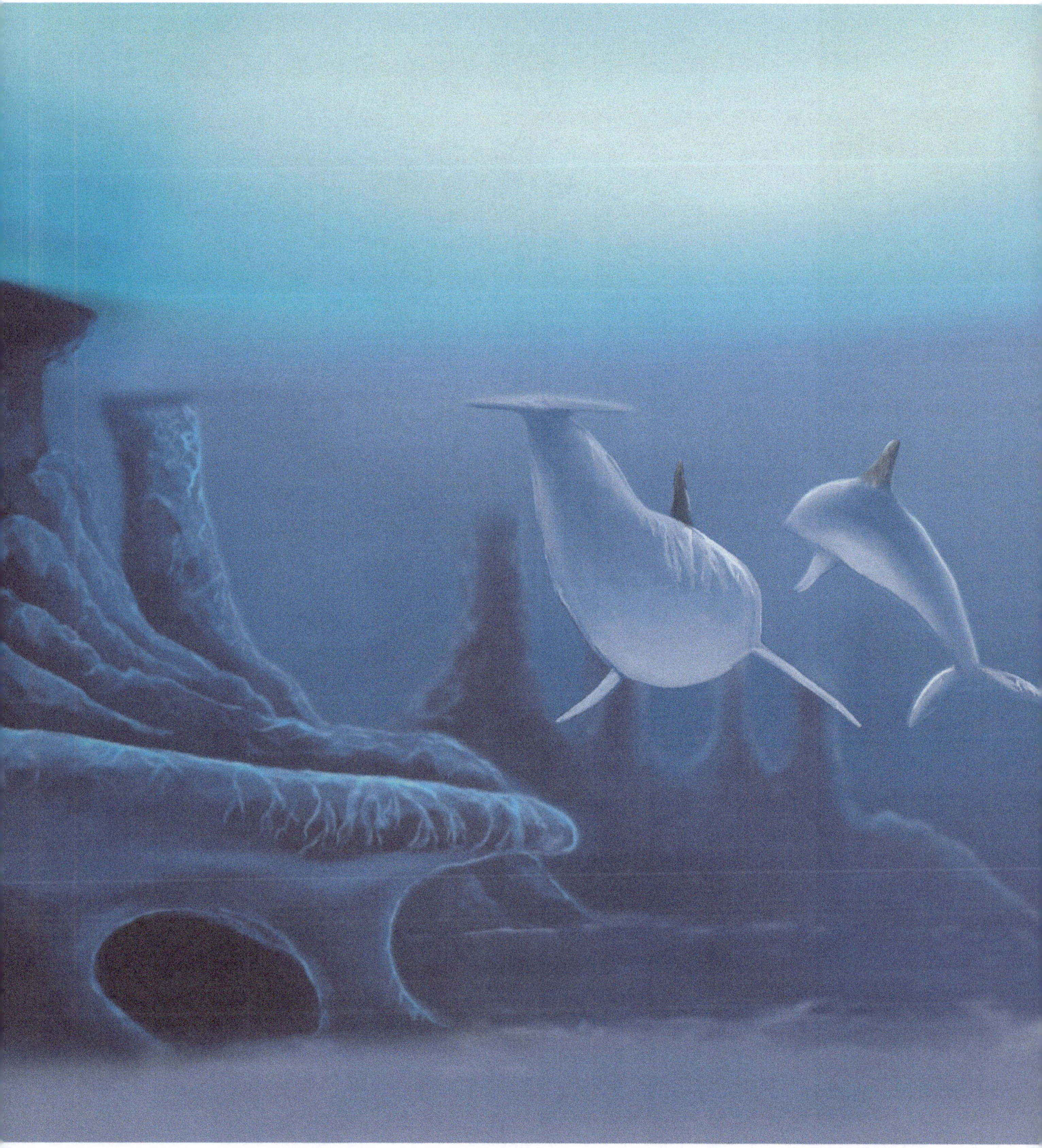

At home, Coty hugs her mother
and reflects, "Behind a treasure I did swim out,
on my journey gaining knowledge and courage.
But there is
one thing I'm sure of now -
that friendship is the greatest of all treasures".

THE END

S SEE HOW MUCH YOU REMEMBER

at is the name of the island where Coty lives?

at do the citizens of the island call themselves?

at does Coty enjoy the most?

ich creature does Coty meet while surfing the waves?

ich animals does Coty encounter on his adventure?

ich animal has three hearts with blue blood?

ich animal advises Coty to follow the trail of seaweed?

ich man-made objects does Coty see his path?

ɔ saves Coty from the sharks?

ich treasure does Coty discover at the end?

9 789356 487819

Printed at Repro India Ltd.